Jo Brand is a stand-up comic with many TV and radio shows to her name. She is married with two children and lives in south London.

Praise for *Look Back in Hunger*:

'As odd things always happen around Jo – ghosts materialise, coat hangers fly out of the wardrobe, pet tortoises attempt suicide – it was a short step for her to decide to train as a psychiatric nurse . . . her world-weary soothing baritone was to be her fortune; she's rightful heir to the comic mantle of Beryl Reid, Joan Sims and Hattie Jacques. Though chunky, what's largest about Jo is her heart, her humanity. I love her'
Daily Express

'Jo Brand is undoubtedly one of the best female comics in Britain and her rise to fame has been monumental . . . Jo's story is honest and very funny'
Sun

'A terrific, uplifting read. South London-born Brand's laconic voice shines through – indeed, you can hear her laid-back delivery in every sentence. The biggest thing about Brand is her heart and her generosity of spirit. She's engagingly light-hearted and excellent company'
Scotsman

'Jo Brand's *Look Back in Hunger* is one of the very best. This is mainly down to the fact that Jo has had a genuinely fascinating life (from psychiatric nurse to one of the country's most loved stand-ups) and her style is engaging, candid and amusing, even when she's talking about some pretty grim stuff. *****'
Heat

'A romp through Jo's formative years . . . Her dry wit shines through'
Now

By Jo Brand and available from Headline Review

Sorting Out Billy
It's Different For Girls
The More You Ignore Me

Look Back in Hunger: The Autobiography

ACT COMEDY SCENE 273
- GET THEM TO CONCUR WITH YOUR WV
  + NEW SET OF COMEDY TARGETS
    (MEN, TORIES, RACISTS, BULLIES)
- COMEDY CLUBS 313-4, 321-2
- 1ST GIG 316-8 (1986)

Jo Brand
Look Back In Hunger
THE AUTOBIOGRAPHY

- THE SEA MONSTER 320
- WEIGHT AS TOPIC IN ACT 328
  + INC SELF-DEPRECATION
- ACT DESIGNED TO SHOCK 330
- <u>FRIDAY NIGHT LIVE</u> 1988

headline
<u>review</u>

First published in 2009 by HEADLINE REVIEW
An imprint of HEADLINE BOOK PUBLISHING

First published in paperback in 2010 by HEADLINE REVIEW

4

Cataloguing in Publication Data is available from the British Library

ISBN 978 0 7553 5525 9

Typeset in Caslon540 BT by Palimpsest Book Production Limited,
Grangemouth, Stirlingshire

Printed and bound in Great Britain by
Clays Ltd, St Ives plc

HEADLINE PUBLISHING GROUP
An Hachette UK Company
338 Euston Road
London NW1 3BH

www.headline.co.uk
www.hachette.co.uk

To anyone out there who hasn't done
what they want to do yet.

Thanks to everyone who helped me.

Contents

Chapter 1
Slaughter in Loughborough

'Please welcome Jo Brand!'

I step into the firing line.

Yes, 'firing line' is the appropriate phrase. The ultimate fear of the stand-up is that a heckle will get you right in the heart and melt you, like the Wicked Witch of the West, into a steaming heap of green gooey stuff.

I am at Loughborough University in the Midlands, notable for its emphasis on sport, which of course I am not. I am doing what we stand-ups euphemistically call a 'student gig'. (In my limited experience this means an inebriated rabble, coated with sexual tension, displaying the concentration span of a gnat, whose milk of human kindness sours quickly and unpredictably, resulting in an avalanche of heckling and/or the appropriation of missiles.)

I am on a stage above the audience and as I look out I see a young male-heavy crowd, probably a bit pissed, gazing at me half expectant, half challenging. And this is what I've sat in a car on the M1 for. Sitting on the M1 is a major hobby of most comedians. The time I've spent on my arse on this charming motorway probably adds up to months, if not a year, of my life.

The M1 is a capricious mistress (yes, I do aspire to be Jeffrey Archer). Of course there are certain times of the week when the M1 is much, much worse, and without doubt Friday is the winner. My heart would always plummet when I looked at a tour sheet and saw Manchester, Sheffield, Bolton, Blackburn or similar booked in on a Friday night, because I knew we would have to leave at a ridiculous time, maybe midday, just to travel a couple of hundred miles. I say 'just' a couple of hundred miles because on a few occasions I drove to Newcastle and back in a day, so Sheffield and the like seem dead easy.

If you put together worst-case scenarios of what can go wrong on a motorway journey, then time stretches like elastic. Maybe Friday night on the M1 with a crash thrown in. If you had road works as well, you knew it was going to take the best part of a weekend to get there.

Service stations weren't up to much in the eighties either, although that staple of the stand-up comic, a Ginsters pie and a can of Coke, was always welcome as far as I was concerned, if only to break the monotony of staring out of the window at the never-changing landscape of scrubby trees and silver-coloured Nissan Micras.

The most demoralising motorway problem is the one when you're tonning it (I beg your pardon, I mean sticking to the national speed limit) back from up north at about two in the morning and out of nowhere there suddenly appears a bleeding massive queue stretching as far as the eye can see ten miles outside London. It makes you want to weep or get out and hit the driver of the car in front, as you've somehow managed to convince yourself it's his fault.

For no particular reason other than I can, here are my three favourite motorways:

The M40

I love the M40. The countryside's glorious and I've never been in a really bad traffic jam on it (although I know many have). I like the sweep down towards Princes Risborough, where a very naughty comedian who'd borrowed his friend's flash motor to take us to a gig once got up to 140 miles an hour, while I screamed because he was a bit of a shit driver.

The M42
There's something glorious about skirting around Birmingham without having to enter the city. Sorry, that was a crap joke at the expense of Birmingham, which I actually like.

The M5
It can be hideous at holiday time, but I'm never on it then so I don't care. Also there are lots of mysterious sculptures at the side of the road which are slightly scary and make you wonder whether, if you broke down there in the middle of the night, the locals might come out and kill you.

And my three worst motorways:

The M1
Everything about it is depressing.

The M56
I once got a puncture on the M56 at two o'clock in

the morning and there was no way I was stopping. I drove into Manchester on it and buggered up my car. Also, I had my car nicked in Manchester and it was used to ram-raid a jeweller's, and that doesn't endear the place to me.

The M50
Where is it going and why is it there?

The lot of the stand-up is to spend hours gazing out of the window feeling that maybe you couldn't get more depressed. And then you meet a student crowd at Loughborough University.

I know it's important to get the audience with the first couple of jokes, because once you start to lose them things can go downhill pretty quickly. I throw out a couple of one-liners, because that's what I do. I ask the audience whether I should move the microphone stand, as otherwise they won't be able to see me. A few people nicked this joke off me subsequently, including some who weren't even fat, and I considered suing them under the Trade Descriptions Act.

I also try: 'I'm anorexic, by the way, because anorexic people look in the mirror and think they look fat . . . and so do I.' Result: some tittering but not the woof of laughter that it normally gets. I think lots of comics cling to their favourite jokes as if they are lifebelts bobbing up and down ahead of them in the stormy sea of a difficult audience. And if you grab for one and the joke goes badly then at that point you start to drown.

I haven't reached the stage where I'm relaxed enough to improvise on a theme or size up the rabble and respond to the mood of the room. Within a couple of minutes it's all gone horribly wrong. Well, it seems like a couple of minutes. For all I know it could be twenty, as I find time has a different quality when I'm on stage – it moves at a completely different pace and when the audience isn't an easy one, it slows down almost to a standstill. The crowd is split. Half of them aren't the least bit interested in what I have to say, turning to each other to chat, and the other half seem quite keen on shouting abuse at me, which on the whole, thankfully, they don't seem to have prepared earlier, owing to its lack of sophistication. Consequently, the air is peppered with a rather uninspiring collection of 'fat lesbians', 'fuck offs' and 'borings', which I can just about cope with, even though it's obviously not the ideal night out for anyone with an ego as fragile as an eggshell.

People constantly say to me, 'Oh God, I couldn't do

your job, you're so brave,' as if I work on an oil rig, do a spot of gun-running in Sierra Leone or tightrope-walk across the Niagara Falls for a living. Honestly though, it's not that bad once you get used to it. I suppose it's possible that my threshold for abuse is higher than other people's. This is partly because I'm a woman, and there seem to be more opportunities for abuse in Ladyworld. We are constantly appraised, commented upon, looked up and down, dismissed as invisible, and all because . . . the lady loves Milk Tray. If you've got a few (or loads) of pounds sewn on due to Milk Tray scoffing, the appraisal is laced with abuse about your unsuitability as a sexual partner. Having had my fair share of this, I kind of expect it and probably put up with more than a three-stone deb with a secure sense of self may have done. Added to that, throughout my nursing career I'd put up with some excessively extreme and very articulate abuse, so a mere 'fat' heckle isn't really much to write home about.

The trick is to try not to take it personally, even though it is directed at you. This involves a shift into a parallel universe which is not too far away, one in which you expect to be abused by an audience and there-fore when it happens you're not surprised and you deal with it.

And you can answer back.

In fact, it's expected of you. Think of all the poor sods working in the helping professions – nurses, ambulance men, doctors, receptionists, social workers and many others – who just have to grin and bear it until they go home and get the chance to take it out on their poor, unsuspecting partner, feet up in front of the telly without any culpability for their other half's frustration and bitterness. As a nurse, I used to tell myself that the people who aimed the most vile and revolting abuse at me were ill (even though lots of them weren't; they were just pissed or horrible) and therefore I shouldn't take it personally. To some extent the same goes for hecklers. I just convince myself they are arseholes. This makes it much easier to come back at them with a well-chosen package of abuse.

Sometimes, however, the friendly neighbourhood heckler is replaced by something altogether stranger and scarier. And Loughborough University is a prime example, as an individual, stand-out voice is added to the wave of insults which is coming at me. It is louder, nastier, more insistent and more threatening than the sum of the somewhat half-hearted attempts at abuse that I have already soaked up.

I hear the words 'ugly whore', 'kill' and 'cunt' in a

surreal swirl of noise. The crowd hears them too and turns towards the voice, perhaps hoping it is a disgruntled javelin thrower who might attempt to skewer me. After all, we are at a sporting university, so it's odds on someone will be good at throwing something, even if it is only abuse. My javelin-throwing days were cut short by a tragic accident in the toilets with a fag and a matchbox. More of that anon. I'd quite like to have a weapon at this point though. I had a recurring dream for a while (sorry, won't keep you too long, I know how dull other people's dreams are) that I got heckled, pulled out a gun and shot the heckler. And the audience fell about laughing. Must have been a club in south London.

I wonder if I'm being heckled by the local serial killer and suspect that my more whimsical attempts at a put-down will fall on deaf ears. So I launch in with my most nuclear of come-backs, and if this doesn't work, I'm history.

'If you don't shut your mouth, I'll sit on your face.'

Yes, I know it's not the height of Wildean repartee, but it normally stops 'em in their tracks. There is a sort of gasped laugh and then I follow it with what I hope will be the killer finisher. (If you're reading this, Mum, you'd better have a sit-down.)

'No, on second thoughts I won't sit on your face, because I haven't got my period at the moment. Doesn't seem worth it.'

Desired effect achieved temporarily. A smattering of applause, quite a lot of laughter and the sound of a small portion of grudging respect winging in my direction.

And then Mr Psycho Trousers starts up again, more vehement, more homicidal and scarier than before. His desire to see me tortured and dead isn't the best compliment I've ever had on stage and even though I can't see him, I conjure up a picture of his screwed-up face, misogyny and murderousness combined to make a photo-fit of seething hatred.

It's strange how much thinking you can actually do when you're on stage facing an audience. The brain ticks over at a hundred miles an hour: planning, pruning material, changing the order, omitting stuff they're not going to identify with, like one's witty five minutes on Delft pottery. While facing Loughborough's answer to Jack the Ripper, in the micro seconds I have available to up my game, I incongruously find myself musing on insults I have received from blokes in the past.Once, sporting short hair and a man's jacket, when walking home from university to my luxury shared flat above a chip shop in West Drayton, a charming rural hamlet near Uxbridge, a lorry driver shouted, 'What's it like being a bloke?' out of his cab at me. I just froze, unable to think of a witty reply, and walked on, head down. Two minutes later, it came to me. I should have walked up to him and shouted, 'I don't suppose you'd know, you creepy bastard' and kicked him in the crossplys.

This is the world of the stand-up. Some sort of superior reply has to be grasped for and delivered in the blink of an eye, and it's bloody difficult to do sometimes. Of course, one's instinct is to just shout the ubiquitous 'fuck off' at them. But crowds these days want more. They want newer, more malevolent put-downs, the verbal equivalent of a blade to the solar plexus.

The combination of Psycho Man's vitriol and the general apathy of the crowd combine to make my temper begin to rise. Why, though?

Haven't I just told you this is the lot of the stand-up? Abuse has to be cleverly parried as we move on to the next joke. Yes, I do believe that, but I also believe there is a limit and as I am beginning to feel as though I am the receptacle for all of this man's hatred towards women, I wonder if this is something any woman should tolerate.

I have always told myself that no performance is worth this sort of emotional pain, even to the point that I get off early and risk losing my money. So throwing out a cheery goodbye along the lines of 'Bollocks to the lot of you!' I exit stage left, rather preferring to be pursued by a bear if the only choice is between it and Psycho Man.

In the dressing room I find my temper is failing to abate and I wish to do violence. This may be due to the several bottles of Pils I've imbibed pre-show as a warm-up ritual, liquid protector and courage inducer. Mark Lamarr, the compere on this occasion and a good friend, is fulsome in his sympathy. I find myself picking up a bottle and heading towards the door to find and do battle with my tormentor.

To my great surprise, Mark attempts to prevent me. A surprise because I'd assumed he'd be right behind me with a bottle the size of Nelson's Column. He sits me down, gets me a drink and counsels me against smashing a punter round the head with a lager receptacle. I'm not happy. Surely this is deserved? As a woman I've had to put up with this (admittedly mostly lower-level) kind of stuff over the years and it frustrates me enormously that there is no opportunity for comeback at all those van-driving-street-roaming-pissed-up arseholes who feel it's their right to comment on women's physical attributes. Surely I am a righteous representative of the female sex, ready to give my all to even the imbalance?

A few minutes later, I begin to see Mark's point. We have discovered the bloke in question is a security man and, apart from thinking that's a slightly unprofessional way for security to behave, I realise the odds of me getting the better of him in a bottle fight are minimal. And so, as the adrenaline begins to flow away to wherever it goes, I calm down and try to put it down to experience, whatever that means.

My Uncle Terry was a bouncer for a while in a club in the northeast. Well, he wasn't really my uncle, thank God, I wouldn't have wanted those genes in the family. He was someone my dad knew from 'a while back' (he never went into details). On the few occasions I saw Uncle Terry – and his appearances were rarer than Halley's Comet – he would entertain us children with rather inappropriately violent tales of punters he had mashed up in some way at the portal of the club where he worked. It's a great job for a misanthrope, and Uncle Terry certainly wore that badge. I think it was safe to say he looked for trouble with the enthusiasm of a fully paid-up member of the psychopaths' league. Most of the tales he related were full of blood and gore squirting out of every imaginable orifice, as he pummelled some poor sod who'd had one too many Babychams and got a bit lairy. I suppose the advantage 'doormen' have is that they are sober and ready for it, while your average pummellee is pissed.

I think my favourite story, the one which stuck in my mind, was of a woman who, having witnessed Uncle Terry giving her escort a good hiding, disappeared for half an hour and then came back and charged at him like a wild animal, brandishing, of all things, a kettle in her hand. Nobody knew whether she'd been home for it, nicked it from a nearby electrical retailer or just happened to find it on the street. It caught Uncle Terry a glancing blow across the top of the head (he could still rather shamefacedly point to the scar) and he tumbled to the ground, at which point Madam poured the contents of the kettle, thankfully not boiling, over his face and gave him a kick in the bollocks for good measure.

Looking back on this, I'm surprised Uncle Terry told us this story, as it doesn't show him in a good light: a tree trunk of a man being floored by a mere woman with the aid of a household implement. But he was tough all the same, like most security men. The one here in Loughborough is no exception.

I wonder to myself: how the blinking hell did I get here and what am I doing? I could be working in a library or pushing a pram round the park. What is my problem?

Chapter 2
Sarf London, Baby

What's the matter with stand-up comics?

Amateur psychologists would have you believe that most of us are emotionally disturbed in some way, having had difficult childhoods rife with incidents of bullying and loneliness. Either that or we have desperately sought our parents' attention unsuccessfully and in adult life are making up for lost time by garnering the adoration of huge numbers of people to compensate for our mums failing to say 'well done' when we came seventh in the egg and spoon race. (That's obviously presuming we are adored which, let me tell anyone considering a career in comedy, isn't a given.)

Obviously, one's early life is not very easy to recall,

as it's a closed book until about the age of five and even after then memories are patchy and fragmented, with some incidents taking on enormous significance and others fading completely from consciousness. Add to this an absolutely appalling memory and my early childhood is a weird hotchpotch of what I can remember (very little) and what my parents and relatives can remember (quite a lot). Therefore what I am about to tell you in this chapter is mostly filtered through the eyes and ears of others.

I popped out quite easily on 23 July 1957, while my father was ushered out of the room looking rather green. I suspect that my poor mother was then regaled with that tedious set of questions that seems obligatory after a birth. Who cares what I weighed? Although it has to be said that it has become a source of interest since I started hauling myself up the few steps on to a stage.

Baby weight has always seemed to me to be a totally dull subject, but it is always the second question asked of a new parent.

1) Boy or girl?
2) What did they weigh?

Why not ask some other completely pointless questions like 'What is the measurement between the bottom of the baby's ear and the bottom of their neck?'

There is, of course, a case to be made for a baby's weight being interesting if it is at the extreme ends of the weight spectrum. For example, a baby weighing nearly a stone is of interest, mainly to the mother, who has to ensure its safe passage through quite a small tunnel that really doesn't cater for that size. And once all your friends have said, 'Bloody hell, that's enormous!' it is the poor mother who has to lie back in agony while some junior doctor practises his embroidery skills on her.

Again, if the baby is a tiny little thing weighing almost nothing, there are obviously health concerns, unless it wants to be a model. Sorry, I'm rambling. Suffice to say, I was neither of these and my baby weight did not presage the horrors that were to come (not in my opinion, that is, but in the opinion of others).

I was born in south London or, as we prefer to call it, 'sarf' London, destined to a life of taunts from those nobs who populate the north side of the Thames and think they're so sophisticated and superior. Little do they realise they pay a high price for this, in that one has to park two miles from one's own house if one lives in north London and one is congenitally debilitated by a damaged brain which forces one to compulsively make the same joke ad nauseam about cabs not going south of the river.

My mum and dad are called Ron and Joyce. My dad was a structural engineer. No, I don't really know what that is either, but as far as I understand, in between periods of going to college, he worked at various building firms as a site engineer and was responsible for such projects as new roofs or office blocks. One of the jobs he did, which I always thought sounded exciting, was a massive hotel block in Dubai. Apparently, the concrete had been mixed up wrong and the entire block was sinking into the sand. So my dad was called out there to devise some way of shoring the whole thing up. I also remember he would be called upon from time to time to go to the scene of something like a motorway bridge collapse and work out what had caused it.

He also happened to be working at Brixton Prison when it was discovered that lots of prisoners were climbing out of a window and going to the pub and then coming back after last orders. I know it's a bit scary to think of all those criminals knocking round Brixton pubs, but there's something really entertaining about the idea, particularly that they actually went back after a sesh.

My mum wasn't anything at this point. I say that, but she was feisty and independent. Let's just say there wasn't much she could put on her CV.

My parents met each other through the Young Socialists, which doesn't seem to have been quite as worthy and dreary as it sounds. From what I can glean, they had a drink, a laugh, the odd meeting and country rambles fuelled by beer, as opposed to the Old Socialists who sat by the fire with a cup of Complan and moaned about the failures of the Communist elite in Russia.

The Young Socialists' official title was the League of Youth and it was based at Clapham Park Road. There was debating, during which I think my mum first caught my dad's eye and ear, because she was one of the few women to get up and join in. In those days a woman with a bit of an opinion to express was rather unusual and slightly frowned upon, as women, to a large extent, were supposed to be decorative and domesticated. There were also table tennis, fundraising dances and public debates with the Young Conservatives – bet that was a hoot. But I know that my mum and dad's favourite activity was the rambling. They would all meet at a pub on Clapham Common on a Sunday morning and then travel by train to a rural destination, get their book of rambling routes out . . . and ramble! The group was anything from five to fifteen strong and they would wander through beautiful countryside, singing songs and having a laugh.

Sounds like quite good fun, doesn't it? Apart from the actual rambling bit, of course.

At this point my mum was seventeen or so and my dad twenty-one. Within a year they were hitched. There were a few hiccups, I think. My mum's dad was very strict and at one point, as family legend has it, chased my dad round the garden waving a shotgun at him. My mum had done very well at school and was lined up to go to Oxford via a scholarship, which, of course, went by the board when she met my dad, thus causing the anger on my granddad's part.

The house into which I was born was a little terraced Victorian place on the Wandsworth Road with an outside toilet. See, I had it rough as a little un (I'm joking), although I don't think I could manage to get out to the toilet on my own for a couple of years, by which time we'd moved anyway.

I was the second child of three, being the girl sandwich in the middle of two boys. And this is what I think set me on the road to a career in comedy and comes loosely under the heading of 'competition'. I never had a sister to point me in the direction of girliness, just two rather wild companions, Matt and Bill, whose major interests lay not in which piece of pink clothing they could don to promenade round town in, but rather which gun they could pick up to take a warning shot at the neighbours. Plastic, not real.

Bill is the oldest, being eighteen months older than me, and Matt is two years younger. As adults they are lovely. Bill is one of those people who is enormously kind and will do anything for anyone to the detriment of his own time. He is also hugely entertaining and an ace joke-teller, preferring to relate jokes that have a proper structure rather than the wild ramblings of the so-called alternative comedian. Matt, on the other hand, is all things musical, an accomplished guitarist, composer and singer. He lives in Germany and I don't see him very much. If they were not my brothers, I would have considered either of them a perfect husband.

However, as children they were a different matter. I saw them as rivals in almost everything we did. Who got the most sweets, who had the most attention, who won at games, who could hit the hardest, who could give the best Chinese burn – everything.

Despite this, and probably due to a somewhat rigid upbringing by my parents, who were sticklers for politeness, I was a NICE LITTLE GIRL with good manners. I do remember a very early incident with a neighbour, when I was probably about three years old, she being not the most hygienic of women, who invited me and my brothers into her hot flat for a drink, which turned out to be a slug of naturally warmed longlife milk served in a cracked, dirty and bluebottle-saliva-ed cup with some ominous-looking bits bobbing up and down in it. Having been taught not to refuse any polite offerings of food or drink, I duly but unwillingly swallowed it and promptly threw it up everywhere as my stomach wasn't quite as polite as I was. Since that day, I haven't been able to be within six feet of longlife milk without being filled with a huge desire to projectile vomit. Hardly a life-endangering condition, I know, but one I feel the need to warn anyone bearing such goods about, in case they are standing in the firing line.

We weren't long in the house with the outside toilet and pretty swiftly we moved a few yards up the road to a bigger house with an inside toilet.

Other early memories are of days full of sunshine playing in the communal gardens with a gang of kids or being squired up to the paddling pool on Clapham Common by one or both of my grandmas to give my mum a day off to lie down and neck a couple of bottles

Jo Brand

of vodka in bed or whatever her hobby was at the time – probably tidying up and washing clothes, I should think.

As a kid, it's all Christmas and birthdays, if you're lucky enough to have decent parents, and one Christmas I got a kitten. Only problem was it had been spooked and legged it up the chimney, refusing to come down, despite some rather amateur attempts to persuade it, ranging from a saucer of milk in the grate to trying to smoke the poor little bugger out by lighting a fire under it.

I was worried. I thought perhaps it would never come down. I even wondered if this was a story the adults had cooked up so they didn't have to actually give us a kitten. When they tried to smoke the kitten down, I thought it might catch fire or choke. So the whole thing was a three-day anxiety fest on everyone's part. We kids rushed downstairs every morning to see if it had appeared or not. And there was a bit of a family history of losing pets. The goldfish had been found floating on top of the water in its bowl and had then mysteriously disappeared (down the toilet as it happens, but we didn't know that at the time) and my grandma's lovely parrot, Gussie, which used to fly around the room during the day, had escaped out of a window to the dubious freedoms of southeast London. To be honest, I didn't expect much and I think that is probably a good mantra for life as you never get too disappointed.

The kitten eventually came down voluntarily and being a little black thing was promptly named Sooty. I realise that in this day and age that name would be totally inappropriate and it illustrates the chasm between today and the 1960s in terms of the approach most people took to race. After all, the first big wave of black people had only arrived in England some few years before and almost everyone was suspicious of them, if not downright hostile. My mum played a trick on my grandma, as she was somewhat outraged by the fact that my grandma had specified that her house should not be sold to 'coloured' people. Upon hearing this, my mother called up my grandma using a West Indian accent to wind her up and informed her she was on her way round to view the house. History has not recorded my grandma's reaction when my mother arrived laughing heartily.

This brings me to an incident in the nineties, when I took part in a benefit in Bradford. I was working with fellow comic and good mate Geoff Green, and the manager of the theatre asked me if it was possible for his friend, a Zimbabwean singer-songwriter, to do a few songs at the beginning of the show. This was all arranged. I was compering from off-stage with a mic. We were corralled in a dressing room in the bowels of the theatre when I heard the singer finish earlier than I'd assumed he would and was forced, in my extremely unfit fashion, to leg it as fast as I could up the stairs to the backstage area, to announce the next act, Geoff. The reason we were in a dressing room so far away from the stage was because we were performing on a Sunday, the only night off for the current show, *Sooty*, all of whose paraphernalia was locked in the dressing room right next to the stage. (For those of you who are too young, you lucky sods, Sooty was a bear glove puppet that appeared on our televisions. He couldn't speak, just nod. Just as well. He was annoying enough as it was. Shouldn't diss him. All kids loved him. Except me.)

Arriving at the mic breathless and hardly able to speak, I grasped for a one-liner to amuse the audience and explain my shortness of breath. It was: 'I'm sorry I'm gasping for breath but I've had to run all the way up from downstairs because that fucking Sooty's got the best dressing room.'

Complete silence. OK, it wasn't the most brilliant

line in the history of comedy, but not even a titter? It then began to dawn on me, with the help of Geoff, that in fact the audience assumed I was talking about the Zimbabwean singer and, bless their little hearts, had refused to laugh at a racist joke.

To say that I was mortified is an extreme understatement, particularly as the story spread like wildfire round the comedy circuit and some people chose to interpret it in a way that made me look like a fully paid-up member of the National Front. It was reassuring, however, that in the space of thirty years attitudes had changed so radically(ish). More on this later.

When I look at photos – black and white, of course – of my early childhood in southeast London, it's like looking at a history book. The women, all dressed in the same uniform of flowery dresses gathered at the waist in summer and tweedy sort of suits in the winter, seem like an alien race straitjacketed by the fashion of the time. Trousers were rare and scruffiness a condition punishable if not by death then by the neighbours' whispers. But behind the facade, stirrings were occurring. My mum, quite a force to be reckoned with, had already started a one-woman crusade to achieve some sort of power. When my dad was conscripted into the army and found out he was going to be sent to Benghazi in Libya, my mum wanted to go too. The only slight problem was one of status. Conscripts' wives were not welcome abroad with their husbands and were supposed to wait dutifully at home, writing letters, polishing the step and generally accepting their lot.

Accepting her lot was not something my mum was comfortable with, and off she went to visit some general or other, managing to secure during that meeting an agreement that she would fly out with my dad and be given accommodation in the officers' quarters along with the much posher wives. This was the beginning, I suppose, of my mother becoming a lifelong role model for me. She refused to sit back in her chair and take what was coming to her, and as I grew up I began to realise that she wasn't like other kids' mums. Feminism hadn't even been heard of at that time, but she was certainly a sister doing it for herself.

I think my mum was unusual because she was what I would call a pre-feminist. Feminist didn't rear its ugly (some would say) head until the sixties, although there were probably lots of women who would have liked it to. The role of women in British society was heavily prescribed. They were expected not to work, to have a family, to be a home-maker and do their best to look pretty. Old etiquette books of the time advise things like soothing your husband when he's had a bad day, speaking in a low, calm voice, having his slippers ready for him. Jesus Christ. All very well for blokes, but how dull for women intellectually. I think my mum, like many other pre-feminists, just wasn't satisfied with this small amount of power. She had a big brain and was interested in politics, the news and all those things that woman were encouraged not to worry their pretty little heads about in the forties and fifties. However, it's much easier to be a feminist if you're a lesbian because men don't cross your orbit in the way they do if you're heterosexual. And things like falling in love happen and, hard as that may be to arrange alongside your feminist views, it is something marvellous that women should not have to forgo. And obviously my mum didn't want to miss out.

My dad had had a pretty closed and somewhat rigid, though warm, upbringing. Socially, I don't think that there was much going on at home – his parents just tended to stick to visiting and being visited by relatives. Also, my dad was a child during the Second World War and was evacuated to Reading, which apparently he was quite disappointed by. This was because when they left London they were not told where they were going and had visions of being housed in a lovely farmhouse on the Dorset coast or similar. You can see why Reading might have been a bit of a letdown. They didn't even have the rock festival then. My dad and his little sister, Rene, were lucky that their mother went with them and eventually their father got a job in Reading, so the family were together again.

I think my dad's always been a sensitive soul and the vicissitudes of the daily rough and tumble of life and work were hard for him at times. This resulted in him feeling down occasionally, although at that point it was no more than that. He just found it hard to cope sometimes. My mum, on the other hand, was tough, like her dad, although I suspect that she struggled with the routine of bringing up a family with no outlet for her intellect. There is a conspiracy among the parents of young children not to reveal to those about to embark on the wonder of having offspring just what bloody hard work it is and how squiring a gaggle of young children through their childhood leaves very little opportunity for what we would call 'me' time. Back then women weren't really encouraged to work and I'm sure thousands of them sat at home, brains seeping out of every pore, longing for just a little break from the daily grind of housework, swings and shops. Taking children to the swings is a bizarre combination of quite dull and extremely stressful. They always want to stay longer than you do, but at any moment could potentially plunge headfirst off the top of the slide and break their necks. Also, if you were hoping for a chat with another grown-up and are accompanied to the park by them, it is almost certain that their children and your children will want to play at opposite ends of the playground, ensuring that you are separated as you watch your children tackling what seems an enormously dangerous piece of equipment while you gaze longingly at your friend fifty yards away who is doing exactly the same thing.

Perhaps the main aim of carers of toddlers, apart from feeding them, washing them, dressing them and entertaining them, is to stop them killing themselves. Toddlers have absolutely no sense of danger whatsoever. In fact, the opposite is true. They gravitate towards danger wherever it may be hiding, be it a main road, a bread knife, some bleach, a scary dog, a precipice, an open window, a saucepan full of boiling liquid, or a container of radioactive material. I often wonder if there couldn't be some Mothercare gadget called Eyes-In-The-Back-Of-Your-Head whereby a series of tiny periscopes strapped on to your head would enable you to see what's going on behind you. This would also be very useful for women walking home alone at night, but of course it would then also need a built-in shotgun.

The weird thing about being a kid is that everything is normal, particularly under the age of five. This is because you don't really have anything to compare and contrast your family life with. So say your dad goes round at home dressed as a gorilla with a tutu on, who's to say that's not normal? How would you know? It's only when you start forming relationships with other kids, go to their houses and talk to them about their lives that you realise that your life is different from theirs.

Our family was, I suppose, pretty traditional. We had three meals a day, we sat down at table to eat, we went to bed when everyone else did and celebrated Christmas in pretty much the way everyone else did, with a tree and some fruit. It's hard to imagine these days that a satsuma in your stocking was a treat.

One day a week the two grandmas looked after us and in the summer we would be taken up to Clapham Common where we could plunge into the paddling pool and run around screeching and laughing. Our grandmas were always slightly less strict than our parents; they let us have more sweets and turned a blind eye to vegetables that were not consumed. There was no sense of either of my parents being harried or pissed off. Apart from in the holidays perhaps. We always went on seaside holidays to places like the Isle of Wight. These memories are just collages in my head of the beach, the sun and endless days of simply enjoying oneself.

My parents, like a lot of other parents at the time, felt that an upbringing in London was not the best way to move forward with three children, so when I was four we did what so many had done before us and jumped into the unknown ... otherwise known as moving to the country.

Chapter 3

Country Life, but not for Posh People

Whenever I've been emotionally blackmailed into a quiz night, the quotations section frequently contains the L. P. Hartley quote from his novel *The Go-Between*: 'The past is a foreign country; they do things differently there.'

Well, to me, the country is another country and as far as I'm concerned they do stuff very, very differently there.

We began our rural idyll in what I would call 'starter countryside' – near enough to London to contain hundreds of commuters and a whiff of city grime.

Initially we moved into a rather isolated cottage just outside a village called St Mary's Platt, in Kent, near Sevenoaks, commuter-belt land. We were a cycle-ride away from school, my brother Bill on his own little bike, me in one of those toddler seats on my mum's bike. Come to think of it, I can't actually remember where Matt was. Perhaps we left him in a hedge and my mum picked him up on the way back.

My dad was commuting up to London every day, doing something manly which I didn't understand when I was four. To be honest, I don't understand it very much now either. He was a structural engineer, as I've said, which is something to do with whether buildings stay up or fall down. He was also a bit of an expert on scaffolding, which I never refer to apart from in relation to ladies' underwear. I think I had a line very early on in my comedy act about Isambard Kingdom Brunel designing my bra.

When we were teenagers my dad actually wrote a book on scaffolding, which sold well to those who were interested in that sort of thing. My dad took the summer off to write it and sat in our garage. Predictably, he got rather fed up being on his own all the time, poring over diagrams and researching the history of it.

I think that's probably when he began to get depressed. Who wouldn't?

A book he has written which I much prefer and which was never published was his autobiography. He writes in a very pragmatic style which is easy to read and he has itemised the major incidents in his life and work. It's fascinating if you're in the Brand family, although searingly dull, possibly, if you're not. I really appreciate him doing it because I have no memory to speak of. It has enabled me to put things in the right order in this book and detail a few bits from my early life with the precision of an engineer, which is not my normal modus operandi.

The cottage we lived in was semi-detached, and next door was Old Bloke With His Trousers Kept Up With String (although it's possible he was only about thirty-five) and his family, who are, and may have been then too, just a blur. There was a very long track up to the house and we were surrounded by a smell that you could taste.

Townies may not know what I'm on about. Around us lay acres of fields containing sprouts, but that wasn't the smell you could taste. I suspect the smell was something that had been sprayed on the sprouts which contained a shed-load of cell-mutating chemicals that invaded one's entire nasal system and probably damaged one's brain.

You'd think this might have put me off sprouts for eternity, but no, quite the opposite. I LOVE SPROUTS. Yes, I know they're a vegetable and they're good for you, but even so, cooked properly they are magnificent. Of course, nine times out of ten they aren't cooked properly and I sympathise with the millions of school children who day after day had to eat something that was the consistency of a urine-soaked cat blanket.

Also, they have an entirely fair reputation for converting you into a wind machine, and most of you won't know just how effective you can be in this field if you haven't tried making sprout curry, a lethal dish invented by my friends Jane and Graham, who, funnily enough, nobody visits very much since that recipe came into existence.

The major incidents that occurred in this isolated spot both involved physical or emotional injury of some sort. In the first case, Bill threw the wheel off a wooden trolley thing quite high into the air and it landed on Matt's head. During that time Matt seemed to us to be a miserable little sod who used to spend a large part of the day snivelling about some perceived insult, his face covered in snot. Therefore it took us a while, as neither of us witnessed the glorious moment of contact between wheel and head, to realise that Matt had actually been hit.

The parental reaction to this injury does not qualify for a place in my memory but I assume stitches were required, and I suppose Bill and I thought, 'Well, at least you've got something to cry about now.'

Matt would have been about four at the time and I suppose, being the youngest, he was pissed off about quite a few things. Firstly, Bill and I were already at school and he was stuck at home all day. We were also able to do more things than him, like run faster, climb more trees and catch more butterflies. The image I have from that time is of him trailing behind us saying, 'Wait for me!' quite a lot, while Bill and I ran ahead, displaying the rather sadistic, uncaring attitude that a lot of siblings of that age tend to have, until they are knocked into shape. Although I don't mean that literally.

Having said that, though, my parents weren't averse to the occasional slap or smack to bring us into line. It seems odd that it is simply not acceptable these days, given that it was a part of my childhood. However, it was not something that happened very often and we would have to be pretty bad for smacking to occur. Eventually the anticipation of it was enough to control our behaviour, although for a small group of kids I knew this was not the case.

One boy in our class, who behaved appallingly by throwing things, stabbing children with his pencil and making a selection of farting noises, was regularly walloped by his dad, who seemed to have the patience of an angry nun. It made no difference to this kid at all. I suppose it's similar to those people who don't seem to be daunted by the prospect of going to prison. I bloody am.

As far as my parents were concerned, if one of us did something like hit the other one or deliberately break something that belonged to them then that would occasionally incur their wrath. There was no good cop/bad cop set-up with my parents. They were both quite happy to mete out the smacks from time to time and, as I remember it, they were both equally terrifying when they were angry.

We were brought up to be polite, well-behaved children, because my mum in particular couldn't bear brattish behaviour of any sort, and I think she believed it was important to demonstrate to others that she was a good mother with controllable children. She also worked very hard to make sure we ate vegetables and fruit. I remember on a holiday in France, when I was perhaps seven or eight, we were all due to go to the cinema to see *Snow White*. Before this, though, we had to have dinner, and I mean 'dinner', which used to be in the middle of the day. At some point during my teenage years it was transferred to the evening, which I presume has something to do with the middle and upper classes. As children, we had breakfast, dinner and tea but these days we have breakfast, lunch and dinner. I cannot quite get used to saying 'lunch'. I hear myself say it and think I sound like a twat, which is strange after all this time.

Anyway, back to dinner on holiday in France. Dinner was always meat, potatoes and vegetables, and in this instance the vegetable in question was cabbage, which Bill absolutely hated. We sat down to eat and we all cleared our plates except Bill, who refused to touch his cabbage. The more he was requested to do so, the more he dug his heels in and refused. I think my mum must have got increasingly frustrated because she told him that unless he ate his cabbage he wouldn't be going to the film.

Whether he thought she was calling his bluff or not, I don't know, but he absolutely refused to capitulate and eventually the limits were reached and he was informed he wasn't going to the cinema. I think he was quite shocked, as he'd assumed she'd never follow it through by denying him such a big treat, which the pictures was then. This, of course, was a bit of a pain because one of my parents then had to stay behind with him while Matt and I trolled off to see the film. I can't even remember which parent now. Probably my dad.

Apart from these rare instances of revolution, we were good at occupying ourselves and playing together, despite random incidences of extreme competition. We spent a lot of time outside, building dens or chucking a ball about, and when we moved to an even more rural setting, we ventured further into the unknown, as it were, spending whole days in the woods.

The other major incident that occurred during this time, I only vaguely remember because I was on the periphery of it. When I recount it you may perhaps understand why my mum and dad didn't sit us down and explain what had happened.

A little way up the track from us lived some travellers, who in those days were referred to as 'gypsies' (or 'gippos' by my dad). I have no idea how many there were — one family, perhaps two. I think most of the time the travellers rubbed along reasonably well with the settlers in the cottages, but one night it all went wrong and my dad and a male neighbour found themselves wandering up the track to remonstrate with them for some unacceptable social faux pas, be it noise, fires or bear baiting (only kidding).

Best intentions to maintain a dignified stance notwithstanding, their avowed peaceable position soon flew out of the window and my dad and the neighbour found themselves being chased back down the track by axe-wielding, angry people. Of course, in the telling, the story has become more exciting, with my dad and the neighbour narrowly escaping with their heads in the most recent version.

I'm not at all sure if the two are connected, but it seems to me that not long after this incident we moved from our lonely spot down into the village of St Mary's Platt and ended up on an estate, the sort of English sixties version of *Desperate Housewives*, with manicured lawns, similar cars on each drive, which were dutifully washed of a Saturday morning, and an army of young families with young children our age.

This was much more village-living than our previous house about two miles away. We had a neat little garden, across which you could see lots of other neat little gardens, all filled with 2.4 children and a mum and dad. Most people went to church and the church fête was a big event in our lives. It was the one opportunity you got to do maypole dancing, which I really used to love, when you clutched your bit of coloured ribbon hanging off the pole and circled the pole, going over one kid's ribbon and under another's to create a sort of plaited effect. Years later I saw *The Wicker Man*, in which a policeman goes to a remote Scottish island to investigate a murder and finds the place mired in ancient medieval customs, and it made me think of maypole dancing and its ancient roots.

Despite the suburban nature of this little estate, it was heaven for my brothers and me because it provided an instant social life, and we quickly formed a small gang who would hang around together at every opportunity.

We spent a lot of time with two girls called Amanda and Fiona, whose mum was very friendly with my mum. Both of them were quite naughty and in some ways alien creatures who would take far more risks than us and say things to their parents that we wouldn't dream of saying or else we'd get a whack. I suppose it was just starting to dawn on me then, at around the age of six, that some parents were more liberal than others, and it was fascinating to see what other kids could get away with. The girls were allowed to have more choice in what they wore, for example. I was given clothes and had to put them on whether I liked them or not.

From a very early age, I suppose, I subconsciously absorbed the message that being a girly girl and dressing to please was not the way forward. So I was mainly to be found in a T-shirt, trousers and plimsolls, while other girls on the estate seemed to make more of an effort to wear pretty dresses and nice shoes. That's not to say I didn't have some nice dresses, I did, but opportunities to wear them were rare and within seconds of putting one on food would be spilled down it, much to the despair of my mum.

On the odd occasion, I baulked at what my mum expected me to wear. At some point she bought me a completely hideous fake-crocodile-skin coat which was white and grey. I remember sitting there staring at it and thinking I could not possibly wear it because somebody would definitely take the piss. But refusing to put it on wasn't even an option, so I just had to grit my teeth and hope no one noticed. Of course, everyone did.

A few girls whose heads were filled with the very important details of what was fashionable that year sneered at my clothes, but rather than feel pressurised into forcing my mum to buy me something acceptable, I just thought these girls were sad and empty-headed, even though it was an ordeal being appraised by them.

My parents, it began to occur to me at this point, were quite rigid compared to other parents. Our television viewing was curtailed much more severely than that of other kids we knew, and so began the relentless pursuit, as it inevitably does, of parity with one's peer group. Some parity, however, was achieved whenever a babysitter came round, which was especially good if it was a Saturday night and *Doctor Who* was on. I'm proud to say that I'm so old that I remember the first Doctor Who, William Hartnell, who looked like a wizened old male crone.

It scared the hell out of me, but I still wanted to watch it. Our babysitter seemed to be the female equivalent of the good Doctor, with her white hair and shapeless old people's clothes. I estimated her age at over a hundred and was always surprised that she knew what a telly was, given that in her youth they probably had only just got hold of the wheel.

On one of these babysitting nights, when the adults were all attending a party together, we were allotted the joy of having many other children to stay. Feeling rather put out that we were not swinging with the grown-ups, one of the older, more precocious girls in our party organised an invasion of the adult shenanigans and in our pyjamas and nighties we crept out past the crocheting babysitter and pitched up at the party. Some swearing happened, I think, and we were all escorted back to our straitjacketed children's bedtime with very little empathy.

My mother was working hard to turn us all into NICE CHILDREN, with modesty and politeness as our constant companions. Occasionally the mask slipped, however. Once I was wandering around in a new outfit and a neighbour remarked, 'You look lovely, Jo.' My reply, not mindful of my mum's attempts, was 'Yes, I do, don't I?'

Lucky me. I remember it as a time of sweets – two pennies to spend every Friday after school at the sweet shop. Doesn't sound much, but you could get a shed-load for that. And if you want to know what I chose, just step into one of those retro, fusty sweetshops and it is all arrayed there, but not quite as cheaply these days.

This must have been in about 1963, the beginning of the revolution that was going to allow women the pill and a bit more of a grasp on the testicles of life.

That women were beginning to squeeze and cause some social, sexual and economic pain to men, who had had it all their way up to this point, can't have gone unnoticed by my mum, who was still a housewife and mother. I would imagine thoughts were already in her head about finding herself a fulfilling position workwise.

One adage that was very much adhered to in our house was that it wasn't good not to finish your dinner, for reasons mainly to do with starving children in Africa who would be only too pleased to get their hands on a plate of semi-regurgitated parsnips. Hence stand-offs with my mum would develop from time to time, owing to my refusal to down something which to me was not far off poison. Perhaps the worst was gooseberries. One of the popular children's jokes of the time was 'What's hairy and goes up and down?' the answer of course being 'A gooseberry in a lift', although later in life it could have been applied to me after a mammoth drinking session, heaving forlornly into the nearest receptacle. But I became obsessed with this hairiness business and the thought of it put me off the whole idea of the innocent gooseberry, to the extent that I flatly refused to consume a gooseberry pie prepared lovingly by my mum. Cue a long stand-off, which she won. I shovelled them down and promptly vomited them on to the carpet at the bottom of the stairs. No gooseberries were seen on my plate ever again.

Pets were foremost in our lives at this time and were all named in relentlessly prosaic fashion according to species. Therefore our hamster became Hammy and a baby hare we rescued from the jaws of some psycho cat became Harold, as Hare-y seemed even then just a little bit too much like Premier League football, in which every poor sod is given the requisite 'y' at the end of his name, such as Giggsy, unless it is too ridiculous, such as Rooney-y.

The admiration I already had for my mum was multiplied by ten when one day young Harold the Hare decided he'd had enough of living in our garden and being pawed by three grubby children and made a break for freedom. He set off at the speed of light and as we children realised he was off and began to cry, my mum went after him, somehow managing, as he leapt over the waist-high fence into the next garden, to follow him over in the style of a professional hurdler and grab his back legs in mid-air. We were dead impressed with her agility, having wrongly assumed before that she was not far off a zimmer frame. The fact that we suddenly realised she could probably do it for England gave her a frisson of glamour in our eyes.

We didn't really have a lot of luck with pets. Our tortoise (what would he be called except Torty?) was not the greatest escapee on the block, but with grim determination he could make it out of our garden if he was given long enough, namely a week, which was the time we took when we went on holiday. Not wanting to lose him and find him several gardens down, we improvised a string harness and attached him to a tree, giving him enough space to roam a bit but not head for the hills.

On our return from holiday, we discovered a poor desperate Torty had obviously pulled so hard at his string that it had broken and flipped him over, and there he was on his back, legs waggling frantically in the air. I suppose he'd not been like that for long or he would not have been waggling in any sense.

My early schooldays are a bit of a blur apart from a couple of stand-out incidents. On my first day at St Mary's Platt Primary, I was understandably full of trepidation, and when we all arrived at our allocated desks in the classroom and were told to sit down, I duly obeyed, only to find myself sitting on the floor, much to the amusement of my new acquaintances.

A boy had pulled my chair away as an extremely funny joke and made me look utterly ridiculous at the age of five. I suspect I stored that up and let some poor hapless heckler have it at some point during my early stand-up days. They liked their jokes at St Mary's Platt. One morning we were all told to undress down to our vest and pants and troop into the school hall for a medical examination. On arrival, arranged in rows before a group of teachers, we were informed that this was an April Fool. About half the kids didn't seem to know what they were on about, and the rest of us were just pleased we'd got off spelling for ten minutes.

I do remember, very vaguely, a broken heart at the age of six. A boy I liked very much indeed, called Andrew, emigrated to Australia and I felt bereft. He was blond, had a nice face and was very sweet-tempered and un-oafish, unlike a lot of the boys, who pushed each other around and seemed to have a mental age several years below the girls. Andrew wrote me a charming letter in his childish hand, saying he would miss me, and we even managed one of those chaste, childish kisses that last 0.03 of a second. As far as I remember, the letter was very matter-of-fact and stated the bald facts. When you're six, you don't really write long heartfelt epistles. I think it said something like: 'I'm going to Australia. I will miss you. I love you. A x'

The letter, of course, has disappeared, but my memory of the kiss hasn't.

Chapter 4

Donkey Days

If you are blessed enough to have happy memories of your childhood, you probably remember one particular place above all others as representational of those faraway days, and Benenden in Kent is the scene that I constantly rewind to in moments of contemplation about my childhood. We moved there when I was about seven or eight, and it was pretty much the perfect Kent village. Life seemed to revolve around the green to some extent: church at the top, primary school on one side, vicarage on the other and post office and sweet shop at the bottom, with a pub either side for good measure.

Initially, we lived outside the village, down a country

lane flanked by woods and fields, in a converted old house which stood next to a large and wealthy looking country pile occupied by a mother and daughter aged approximately seventy and fifty. They were posh, and we knew they were because they said 'dunkey' instead of 'donkey'.

Our house had a massive garden leading down to some woods with a stream running through it and Enid Blyton (or to contemporise it a bit, JK Rowling) could have constructed a decent story round the myriad opportunities for adventure contained in it.

I think at this point in time my mum wasn't too happy. The house was isolated, and with two posh old girls next door, there weren't many opportunities for socialising nearby. The house was a long way from any social centre, so my mum was stuck on her own in the house all day. I know I would have gone slowly mad and I assume she did too.

It's strange when you're a child because your parents tend to look older than Old Father Time himself. I think at this time my mum was only thirty, but in my eyes she looked about sixty-five. Also, in the sixties, older women tended to wear what I consider 'adult' clothes and the gulf between them and younger people was very visible. So I remember my mum in a selection of tailored dresses and skirts: in the summer pale, checked dresses with a white collar and in the winter sensible jumpers and skirts. She had short dark hair cut in a utilitarian style, didn't wear make-up unless she was going out and had sensible country-type, lace-up shoes. Lots of the other mothers were a bit more decorative. The perm was king, but thankfully my mum didn't cave in because I've always thought they add at least ten years on, as well as making you look like a poodle.

My mother may have been unhappy, but my brothers and I were only too happy to dive headfirst into this glorious rural playground, consisting as it did of trees to climb, water to fall into, grass to run around on, animals to spot, ropes to swing on and long days during which we would disappear, only returning to the house for meals.

We attended the village school on the green, and it was there I first encountered teachers I did not like, whom I thought were unkind and didn't really seem to like children. It's always hard as a child to get your head around bad adults. The rigid teaching method of some of the teachers was manifested in a number of ways – with sarcasm and cruel comments, and the threat of and occasionally actual violence. There was a sporadic atmosphere of menace which kept our excessive behaviour in check, apart from the odd deviation by the more daring kids.

I remember one child who had a reputation for naughtiness once being told to go and get his shoe bag from the cloakroom and the rest of us watched in fascinated horror as it was swung high in the air several times before making contact with various parts of his body, the net result being more humiliation than pain, carried out as it was in full view of the class. My older brother Bill's class were all lined up outside one day and caned one by one, because one child would not own up to some minor misdemeanour. Once I asked twice in the same lesson to go to the toilet and was informed by the teacher that I would have to bring a potty into school. With the laughter of the class resounding in my ears, I seethed with shame and hated this teacher from that day forward. It was a more effective punishment than a slap round the legs with my own shoe bag.

But, all in all, I think I was pretty well-behaved and a good pupil. I was very rarely in trouble. Not because I was afraid of the teachers particularly, but I was terrified of doing something wrong and it getting back to my parents, who would have come down on me like a ton of bricks. I had lots of friends, felt confident and happy and was very keen on sport. We played sports on the village green and I remember rounders being my favourite. There was nothing quite as satisfying as giving that hard red ball a resounding thwack and making it all the way round the posts while some hapless child legged it out to the edge of the green to try to retrieve the ball.

We played lots of different games in the playground, skipping being a favourite of most of the girls, and skipping games became quite complex, involving running in and out of the rope while two girls chanted some rhyme or other which I now can't bring to mind. Hopscotch was another one and I'm surprised that we never got bored with the endless routine of chucking a stone and hopping up and down the grid, but we didn't.

When I was a kid we had proper weather too, of a non-global-warming variety, and I can remember struggling into school in deep snow to find crates of school milk warming gently on the radiator. They were such sweet little miniature bottles, they looked as though elves had delivered them. In the winter, if the bottles froze, the tops would be forced up, so the bottles looked like they had little hats on. I'm just warning all my family and friends that this is the kind of crap I'm going to refer to endlessly when I'm old and trapped in some residential home, so you may not want to come and visit me.

School consisted of a fair bit of rote learning, punctuated by playtime. I must be one of the few kids who never really came across any bullies in the playground. On the whole, we all got on very well. It was some of the teachers I wasn't so keen on. Perhaps the most dramatic incident I witnessed in the playground involved my brother Bill, who one day during the winter slipped on some ice and banged his face badly (in those days Health and Safety only extended to not allowing sawn-offs to be brought into school). The result of Bill's contact with the ice was that he went into some sort of shock and began to vomit, very impressively, through his nose. He was the talk of the school for days. I just wish that impressing one's peers was that easy when you're grown up, although at a certain age, when group holidays to cheap European destinations are what you crave, vomiting through any orifice comes fairly high on the How To Impress Your Friends list.

School dinners were always a source of physical pain back then. Choice was a much derided concept, as were vegetables cooked in under four weeks. Stews and meat pies seemed to consist of all the bits of an animal it makes one shudder to think of. They were always hidden within a glutinous mass of what was laughingly called gravy and so the satisfaction (or otherwise) of seeing what you were about to consume was denied you.

My mother, revolutionary that she was, once told me that her school meals were so appalling that one day the girls all decided to refuse their meal. By the end of the afternoon the weaker ones had peeled off, caved in and eaten their cold dinners, just leaving my mum sitting alone in glorious ignominy.

My mum went to school in south London, a Catholic girls' school, strict and regimented by the sound of it. I think she always challenged the blind authority that the nuns imposed and resented the slightly sadistic nature of the nuns who taught her. It's a cliché to say it, but why do the vast majority of the women who choose to get married to God end up being frustrated, evil old bags who seem to take a delight in putting the boot in? Their behaviour isn't Christian by any stretch of the imagination, and the many Catholics I've spoken to who ended up working on the comedy circuit all say the same thing – that their lives were blighted by the cruelty of the nuns/monks teaching them. My mum rejected Catholicism while she was a schoolgirl because of what she observed first hand, and so we were not brought up to be Catholic, which I am grateful for. In order to become a comic I had to create my own emotional disturbance rather than have it imposed upon me.

We never refused the appallingly badly cooked first course at school for fear we would be denied pudding. I loved most puddings. They were possibly about 12,000 calories a throw, but they compensated for the cow's perineum under a blanket of pastry you had just forced down. My three top puddings were:

Gypsy tart
Gypsy tart was sublime. It was a kind of sticky, light-brown goo in a pastry case, and I have often searched for the recipe in order to recreate it. I think it was made out of brown sugar and condensed milk which had been boiled and reduced down until it became almost solid. I have done some rather meagre research on whether other people I know had gypsy tart at school and although I've come across a handful, it seems it was only served to children who went to school in Kent. You could feel your arteries clogging up while you were eating it.

Jam roly-poly

What can I say? The name is enough to make you fall in love with this pudding, a kind of superannuated Swiss roll, made with suet to give it a heavy, lardy feel, which would sit in the bottom of your stomach and make you feel sleepy and apathetic all afternoon. Tasted bloody marvellous though.

Apple crumble

A very difficult pudding to mess up. The crumble was always a bit thicker than the fruit contained underneath, just the way I like it!

Unfortunately these spongy puddings were always served with that standard school accompaniment, lumpy custard, which all but ruined them for me. So I developed a painstaking way of raking the custard over the pudding so that it was thin enough to identify the lumps, which I would then remove and dispose of, sometimes into a handy tissue, if I had one, which I didn't very often, or I would just smear them under the table. Yum.

Similar to custard in some ways, and a horror for me, was pink blancmange. I never knew what it was supposed to be – strawberry, raspberry or what. It could have been beetroot for all the flavour it had. The worst thing about it was the thick layer of skin on top. It would have been fine if it could have been lifted up, like a blancmange blanket, and deposited somewhere, but the cooks always seemed to make sure it was broken up and stirred in, so every mouthful had a little or big lump in it. It still makes me feel slightly sick when I think of it.

Despite it being the major part of my day, I remember school as a tiny element in my life as an eight year old.

There was so much to do out of school, and a typical weekend day would find my brothers and me out in the woods with our wellies on, hitting each other with sticks, building a precarious bridge over the stream or chasing each other wildly through the woods. One day either Bill or Matt trod in a wasps' nest, resulting in an extreme temper-tantrum by the wasps therein. Out they came, like cartoon wasps, buzzing wildly and looking for revenge. At this point immediate decisions had to be made and I ran one way and the boys the other. Thankfully for me, the wasps decided they wanted male flesh and as I ran I could see the swarm chasing them. But as many of you will concur I'm sure, the pain of one's siblings when you are a child is a source of great delight on the whole, and when I arrived home, having hidden in a big tree just to check they weren't after me, I found Bill and Matt stung pretty badly, bemoaning their fate, which gave me a great deal of pleasure. I'm sure my mum must have despaired that she was raising a psycho daughter at that point and, of course, with hindsight, I realise it is shocking to revel in your brothers' pain. It just goes to show that the cauldron of sibling rivalry and the intense hate it engenders at that age is something alien to adult analysis. Bill and Matt were constantly taunting me, pinching me, whipping me with bendy sticks, pushing me off gates, and so when they got it in the neck . . . enormous pleasure for me.

My dad rented a field up the lane while we lived at this house, which added another layer of joy for us. In the middle was a pond with fish and the field itself was surrounded by woods. It seemed huge to me, being seven acres, the size of about eight football pitches.

At one point during our childhood we were given for an hour or so a baby to look after who belonged to my mum's friend Margie. I've no idea why on earth that baby was put in the charge of three children between the ages of six and ten, but she was, and we were allowed to take her off up to the field for a walk, wrapped in her charming, downy white blanket. We took turns holding her and I have to say we took liberties with that poor child, occasionally stopping to play catch with her along the way. She loved it, however, and giggled her head off as she was propelled a short distance through the air into the arms of a waiting child. When we got to the field, we thought we'd show her the pond. It was slap-bang in the middle of the field, surrounded by trees, and had a small jetty poking out into the water. Bill used to fish off it.

I think our original idea was to dangle her feet into the pond, another attempt at trying to make her laugh. So we went out along the little jetty, as the banks were a bit muddy and tended to give way. One of us, I can't remember who, held her off the end of the jetty and attempted to dangle her down into the water. But it was quite difficult to hold her, the grip loosened and she sploshed into the pond. She was immediately grabbed and pulled out before she could float off or sink and we carried her back home in a right state, smelling of pond water. I can't remember how we explained it, but I know we didn't actually confess to the fact that we'd dropped her – that would have been no sweets for a couple of years. Not my finest moment of childcare, and it's a good job I didn't include that on my CV when I applied for a job at Barnardo's later in my life.

As if having our own field and pond wasn't enough, a local woman asked my dad if she could put her three donkeys in the field for a while. They were a mother and two sons, rather inappropriately named Rag, Tag and Bobtail. They were not particularly tame, and we spent hours playing Wild West-type games trying to lasso them with my mum's washing line. We accidentally discovered that if you touched the top of their tails, it sent them slightly mad. Cue invitations to all the local kids, who would gingerly haul themselves on and then find themselves haring down the field, clinging on for dear life, once the 'touch tail' method was employed. Their journey would normally end when whichever donkey it was bucked them off into a big patch of mud. Superb entertainment.

My brothers and I continued to challenge each other at every possible opportunity, and on one occasion I was sitting on a half-open five-bar gate at the top of the field when, for a laugh, they pushed the gate, sending me toppling backwards and ripping open the underside of my arm as I descended, on some handy rusty barbed wire. As you can imagine, it really, really,

really hurt, but something inside me prevented me from crying in front of my brothers. Once they saw tears falling, they saw that as some sort of victory. So I did anger and swearing instead, the sort of swearing you do when you're eight, which is normally something along the lines of 'You buggering fuck!' because you're not quite sure how to put the words together for maximum shock effect. It all ends up being slightly humorous. I went off home on my own, saying I could manage, and once out of sight of my brothers, I cried my eyes out. Not only was there pain, but the sight of half of the inside of my arm hanging out, most of which appeared to be made of yellow marmalade, made me cry even more. A visit to the local casualty department ensued and I still have a charming scar to remind me of that day.

Despite the fact that the house next door was inhabited by two old ladies, it was of great interest to us, because we'd heard it was haunted by a ghost called Kitty Fisher (yes, the very same one from the nursery rhyme 'Lucy Locket Lost Her Pocket'). A lapse in manners occurred again, much to my mother's embarrassment, when we cornered the younger of the two ladies and asked if we could stay the night and see the ghost. Weirdly, she agreed, so despite my mother's attempts to reverse the invitation, we set off one evening in our pyjamas to the haunted house. We'd all been put in the same bedroom and I don't mind admitting I was shit scared. I think my brothers were displaying a bit more macho bravado than me and eventually, after much giggling and ghost noises, we dropped off to sleep.

In the middle of the night I woke with a start and what felt like a cold hand clutching at my heart and promptly fell out of bed. It was pitch black, so I staggered to where I thought the door was and found my way out into the hall. Up above me, with a ghostly light above her head, was Kitty Fisher. Well, I wasn't staying around, either to see what she would do or to save my brothers. With a squeal, I legged it down the stairs, out through the front door and across two gardens to the safety of our house. My brothers slept on oblivious and when I returned the next day to see if they had been murdered by the ghost, I was taken up the stairs and shown a big portrait of a woman on the wall with a light over it. Voilà, one ghost.

Whether this was responsible for my parallel career as a scaredy-cat, I don't know, but I have remained utterly averse to darkness and the horrors contained in it. During my university years, I once watched an appallingly scary film called *Black Christmas* with Jane (she of sprout curry fame) and so terrified were we after it had finished, we slept in the same bed with the light on all night. A vivid imagination is a complete curse in circumstances like this and I trace it all back to that bloody Fisher woman in my childhood.

Chapter 5

Anorak Bullfighting

Eventually – at my mum's behest, I'm sure – we left behind the old house in the middle of nowhere and moved slap-bang into the centre of the village of Benenden, to a white weatherboard house at a crossroads, next door to the butcher's shop.

At this point my dad was working as a lecturer up in London, so he was commuting on the train every day. This meant that he was out of the house from roughly seven till seven, and so it was a relief, I think, for my mum to be in the village, where at least she could pop out and talk to people other than two charmingly bonkers posh old ladies.

This was when my dad came to be known as 'Old

Man Brand', even though he was only in his thirties. He acquired this title because diagonally opposite the house was a sort of memorial/shelter thing that attracted some local bikers and general layabouts of an evening to share a can of beer, and my dad spent some considerable time shooing them off in a fairly vocal way. Although they never fought back like the 'gypsies' at St Mary's Platt, it was a familiar scene as my father left the house to remonstrate with the gang in a politely threatening manner.

At that time my mum and dad owned a pair of Renault cars, both of which were notoriously difficult to start in the winter. Thankfully, the crossroads were at the top of a hill, so almost every morning when it was cold the ritual of pushing both cars to the top of the hill and jump-starting them on the way down was a familiar one. For some reason, they never let us kids have a go.

School continued to be good fun, although the gruesome prospect of growing up was never far away. One day a somewhat precocious girl called Hannah showed me a pair of pants with a towelling gusset she was wearing and explained that this was because it wouldn't be long until she and all us other girls would have 'blood coming out of our bottoms'.

Well, I was appalled by this and refused to believe it, allowing this piece of unpleasant information to sink to the back of my mind.

Boy/girl relationships encroached at an early age. When I was about eight, a male student teacher taught at our primary school for a while and some of the girls seemed mighty excited by his presence. He used to give the girls a ride on his bike, and the aforementioned siren Hannah was always first in the queue, doing what I think was eight-year-old flirting. I wasn't in the slightest bit interested and would always decline his offers of a ride.

I've always been crap at flirting. It's always made me feel slightly queasy watching other women flirt, as it's not a language I've ever really been conversant in. Having two brothers and, I suppose, being a 'tomboy' (what a lot of people would consider a trainee lesbian), it didn't seem like a satisfactory method of communicating with males to me. I'd rather have hit them with a stick or made them laugh.

One of my best friends at primary school just happened to be the daughter of someone involved with the local church. This meant that I felt compelled to go every week, because she did. Apart from Harvest Festival, when some good hymns were sung, church wasn't really my cup of tea. The language seemed archaic, the sermons were coma-inducing, and a lot of the so-called Christians in church didn't seem to me to be very Christian elsewhere. I suppose I had developed a view of Jesus as a bit of a social worker/socialist and the last thing some of the church-goers seemed to be was altruistic. I tried to work out a way of going without actually being there. Princess Anne was in the choir for a short while and as I had already developed republican tendencies, I didn't fancy that. Finally, I alighted upon the perfect solution: bell-ringing. This would mean I'd have to be out of the main body of the church and could avoid the rest of the service, as we didn't finish until seconds before it started.

Bell-ringing is hard work and quite dangerous. I won't go into the finer details of it here, because you may slip into a coma, but suffice it to say, it's not just about pulling a rope with a fluffy bit on it.

Someone, I can't remember who, regaled us with tales of some hapless bell-ringer breaking his back on the ceiling of the bell-ringing chamber, so I was wary at first. When I started to relax a bit, that, of course, was the best time to play a trick on me. We were in the process of 'bringing the bells down' one day (or was it 'up'? I never could remember) when one of the younger bell-ringers (most of them were about ninety) said very casually to me, 'Hold this a minute, will you?'

Without thinking or looking, I stuck my hand out to grab the rope and found myself being propelled upwards at an alarming rate. How high I went, I really couldn't say, but in my mind it was about twenty feet. Through my head ran the story of the bell-ringer with the broken back but, serendipitously, before I could find out whether I was to be Broken Back Number Two, I instinctively let go and plummeted to the floor, sustaining just a sprained ankle and a red face at having let myself be fooled. Everyone pissed themselves laughing apart from a few sensible elders who remonstrated with the young joker about the potential danger he had put me in.

The cynicism I felt at an early age about the church and its representatives was amplified by the behaviour of my friend's father, who seemed to me to be batting for the other side (religiously, not sexually). It felt to me as if he was taking every opportunity to humiliate me. Once at a party, when we were playing Blind Man's Buff, he poked me and took the piss, to the great amusement of my peers, and once, amazingly, during my first communion, when I took the wafer, he called me a 'greedy little girl'. I was shocked. Did God really sanction this sort of comment at such an important moment? I was sure that he didn't.

One of my favourite pastimes when I was about eight or nine was a version of bullfighting. There was an open area at the top of the village green called Hilly Fields (yes, sometimes they're not very imaginative in the country) and I used to go up there with a friend and try to bullfight the heifers. I had a red anorak which sufficed for waving at them and although I didn't realise it at the time, the reason they ran at us was more out of curiosity than the red-rag-to-a-bull thing. Of course, we would start running away screaming almost immediately and were never in danger of being gored, mainly because they didn't have any horns.

The version I play of this these days, if I'm walking across a field of young cattle, I like to think of as 'Bullock Roulette', which involves trying to get past them (sneaking or running) without being surrounded. My dear Uncle Les used to say that if you stand still they will screech to a halt just before several tons of flesh and bone slam into you. I was never able to quite trust him on that.

My Uncle Les was a lovely Herefordshire man, one of the most, if not *the* most, charming and delightful men I've ever met. Versed in the ways of the country, he was originally a farmer and after that he managed an estate for a posh bloke. A fount of knowledge on country matters and always accompanied by a faithful Labrador, he'd be striding through the forest or skirting the edge of a field in his wellies. But along with the rugged exterior of beard, sun-reddened skin and horny hands, he was such a gentle, softly spoken, sweet-natured person. One evening he took me to watch badger cubs playing in the early evening.

Village sport was always a big deal when I was a kid, but revolved mainly around the male of the species. My brothers both played football and were that breed of Manchester United fan who's never set foot in Manchester. I was encouraged to support West Ham, which I was happy to do, because my hero was the blond and endlessly wholesome Bobby Moore. Every time they lost, which wasn't infrequently, I would be smacked about a bit or teased to the point where I had to slap *them* around a bit. Girls weren't encouraged to play football at the time. I suspect if we'd tried we would have been incarcerated in a wicker man and ignited. I spent a lot of time, therefore, watching my brothers play football and my dad play cricket. My poor old dad had a singularly unsuccessful cricket career, only playing twice for the village team. On one occasion he was out for a duck and on the other a golden duck.

I'm at the sort of age when the saying 'Do you remember where you were when JFK was shot?' applies. This has since been replaced for some by Princess Diana. Strangely, I can remember where I was when *Bobby* Kennedy was shot – watching my brothers play football at the rec, or recreation ground to give it its full title – but not JFK. In case you are interested: Princess Diana – in a motel on the M1, on my way to compete in a rally-driving event.

Yes, rather foolishly, in my late thirties, I took up rally driving. I had always liked driving fast, especially round London, and found myself revving up at traffic lights if ever I was next to a likely-looking lad in something powerful. I got my international licence through a series of rallies all over the country with John, who was my tour manager at the time. He was a very fast driver too. The only drawback for me was having to wear a ridiculous Michelin Man rally suit, in which I did actually look like a Michelin Man who'd had a sex change. And you couldn't go for a piss in it without taking the whole thing off. It is these minor details which destroy promising careers in so many fields, I am sure.

Over the years, cars have been a source of pain and joy. I haven't owned many and they have ranged from the sublime to the ridiculous. Starting off with a baked-bean can on wheels (more later), I have driven two Fiat Pandas and an Uno. I ran some poor little kid over in the Panda, when she ran straight out in front of me on a steep hill in Camberwell. She looked about eight and her head hit the wing mirror. I immediately leapt out of the car to see if she was OK but she was either so shocked or I was so frightening that she legged it and I couldn't catch her. Made me very proud to know I couldn't run faster than an eight year old.

I briefly dabbled in crime in the village of Benenden. Firstly, my best friend Linda and I were caught by the local bobby cycling down a lane, two on a bike. As he didn't really have much to do, I presume, he made rather a big deal of it, stopping us, lecturing us and, if I remember rightly, writing something down in a note-book with the obligatory stubby pencil that doesn't work unless it's licked several times. We listened patiently to his monologue, waited for him to cycle off round the corner and immediately got back on and continued our journey. Unfortunately, he had the measure of us and had obviously decided to see whether we'd obeyed him or not. He sneaked up behind us to redeliver his lecture at double the volume. As soon as the words 'tell your parents' were ejected from his mouth we knew we were in trouble, being kids who were more scared of our parents than a policeman. Is that a good thing? I presume so, unless your parents are criminals trying to lure you into a life of crime. In fact, I don't think he did tell our parents, wisely deciding that the threat was enough to scare the daylights out of us.

My second crime involved stealing some sweets from the village post office. Temptation became too much when I realised I'd spent all my pocket money and was forced, while others purchased Fruit Salads and the like, to stand and watch without getting satisfaction. So I took the risk and grabbed a handful when I thought the shopkeeper wasn't looking. She, however, possessed the unsettling physiological power of 360-degree vision and, to my horror, I was stopped on the way out of the shop. This time I'm afraid my parents were involved, despite my attempts to persuade her that it wouldn't happen again and therefore we could just forget about it. I suspect the degree of reaction I got from my parents (excessive) was more to do with the embarrassment I'd caused than the seriousness of the crime. Suffice it to say, they didn't seem proud of my skills.

Since then I don't think I've committed any serious crime, apart from perhaps some very grave fashion faux pas.

The rest of my primary school days were filled with navy-panted sports days, muddy shenanigans in various wooded settings, Brownies (not brownies, I don't think those delicious offerings had made it over from America by that point), church fêtes, sunny days, snow, playing and living a life untouched by the horrors of the world.

And there were, of course, holidays and visits to the seaside. By that point both sets of grandparents lived by the sea, my dad's parents in Hastings and my mum's parents at Selsey Bill. So there were many days spent on the beach in cloudy, windy weather, stabbing at the pebbles with a spade and being tormented by wasps.

My major memory of Hastings is my granddad standing on a breakwater in his swimming trunks shouting, 'Watch this, kids!', diving in, hitting his head on a rock and coming up out of the murky green sea with an enormous cut on his head. We all tried not to laugh at first, but when we realised he was going to be OK, we laughed a lot.

Holidays were mainly taken in England. We spent one summer, although it could have been winter it was so cold, in Snowdonia and one day my dad and I decided to scale Snowdon. My brothers wimped out for some reason I can't recall. So we set off with very little except some water, my dad reassuring me that there was a cafe at the top where we could have a good old stuff. On our way up, we heard a long and chilling scream and subsequently discovered someone had fallen and been killed, a terrible experience I couldn't get out of my mind for months.

The horrors of the world did occasionally surface, when my brothers and I discovered where my parents hid magazines and papers considered to be too painful/ violent/rude for the consumption of children, but I kind of wish we hadn't. Holding all that off for as long as possible would have been the preferred option.

Chapter 6
Disgusting of Tunbridge Wells

So I left primary school behind, but not with a heavy heart, because I was excited about going to big school. I had passed my eleven plus, that ancient exam which we had in the old days that weeded out the brighter kids. Unfortunately, our nearest grammar school was twenty-five miles away in Tunbridge Wells and involved a two-hour journey each way. My mum and dad didn't want me to sit on a bus for four hours a day, so they arranged for me to go to the local comprehensive, a mere five miles or so away.

I started at this school and settled in well until an

incident occurred which changed the way I felt about the place.

Before I started secondary school I had been learning to play the violin. At the time it was a bit of a chore. I had also learned to play the piano. My Grandma Grace, my dad's mum, had been pretty musical and could bash out a few well-known tunes on the piano, and my dad had learned the violin at school and toured with the school orchestra, so it seemed natural that I learned to play instruments as well. My dad's old violin would occasionally be brought out and sawed away at. The problem with a violin is that unless you are Yehudi Menuhin (for older readers) or Vanessa Mae (for younger ones) the playing of the violin alone, without any accompaniment, is not a pleasant experience. It sounds hideous to my ears and something that should only be done in front of relatives you would quite like to go home early.

So although I did like music, and I loved some of the classical stuff my dad played on Sunday mornings, I knew I could never aspire to it, so it was all a bit depressing. I had had piano lessons in the nearby town with a white-haired old lady called Miss Blount, and although she was pleasant, she didn't fire me up with the requisite passion to be a brilliant pianist. I plonked away at 'Greensleeves' and the like, and I'm sure it was only my parents who stood there proudly while I faltered through stuff. Everyone else who was forced to listen to it probably couldn't wait to escape.

My brother Matt was the musical one, but at the first opportunity he moved off the piano and taught himself to play the guitar. Later on, when he lived in Germany, he was in a band for a long time that looked like T-Rex after a spell in the trenches. He never made it as a pop star, which is the fantasy of all teenage boys, but he is one of those people who can pick up a guitar and knock out a few tunes you can sing to, which is a useful skill.

Anyway, back to the incident. Unbeknownst to me, the staff at my new school, wanting to get more kids to take up instruments, had plotted with my violin teacher a way of demonstrating the joy of learning music. I turned up at school one day with my violin for a lesson, only to be told I was playing in assembly in front of the whole school. I could have done with a TARDIS at this point, as the prospect filled me with horror, and, true to expectations, it went as badly as it possibly could. I shook, I sweated, I went bright red and I sawed away at the bloody violin producing a sound that grated worse than white noise. The audience, on the other hand, shuffled their feet, giggled, snorted, yawned and blew the occasional raspberry, the subtext of which was 'You uppity, talentless, show-offy, middle-class little twat.' I was mortified and wondered if I could ever walk among them again with my head up. To punish my teacher for this abasement, I gave up the violin and stood fast against his pleas to reconsider.

The rudimentary sex lesson we had at this point was somewhat traumatic too. We were informed of the very basic mechanics of menstruation, which was made to sound like some ancient medieval torture and unsettled me enormously. I went home that day and remarked to my mum that I was so thankful we only had to go through it once. My mum informed me that I'd obviously misunderstood and was looking at a lifetime of it. I didn't get over this piece of earth-shattering information for months. Subsequently, I have been accused by the more upmarket tabloids of only ever talking about periods, in my quasi-feminist, man-hating way, and I would just like to point out (for any tabloid journalists reading this, which is unlikely) that out of probably nearly twenty hours of stand-up material there is roughly ten minutes of material on periods, which hardly qualifies as 'talking about it all the time'. So there!

Not long after that, the school contacted my parents and said they wanted me to go up into the third year from the first year as I wasn't being challenged enough. I had really enjoyed myself at the school up to that point. I didn't find the work particularly easy or feel different from my peers. I always looked forward to going to school and I would have been quite happy to stay there for the rest of the allotted time, despite the violin incident. But this was a social minefield. My old peers would hate and resent me, as would my new peers. My parents caved in. I think they were aware of how difficult it would be for me to be in a class with kids two years older – the potential for bullying and the sense of alienation generally – and although they were very unenthusiastic about me spending four hours a day on a bus, it was the lesser of two evils.

They decided to send me to Tunbridge Wells Grammar School for Girls after all. At the time I wasn't that keen to go because I was happy where I was. I didn't have any feelings one way or another about the grammar-school system. I think the fact that it was an all-girls' school was in some ways more of a chal-lenge, as I had been used to being at a mixed school. Although boys weren't my favourite things when I was twelve, I think in hindsight it was important for them to be around, as growing up with boys and spending all your schooldays with them gives you a more natural perspective on them and makes them seem less like alien creatures. They become alien creatures when you're a bit older.

So, on my first day, I found myself waiting at the bus stop at 6.45 a.m., freezing cold, in the regulation navy-and-yellow uniform (yum) with a ridiculous felt hat. We were transported to Tunbridge Wells by an ancient, wheezing double-decker bus which stopped at about a hundred villages on the way. After a few weeks I had got into the routine – our hats stayed off until we reached the outer environs of the town, at which point we suspected a teacher/border guard lurked, furnished with binoculars, to pick off those naughty girls who didn't have their hats on. Some years later, fags were added to the mix, as the bravest of us sat at the back and puffed inexpertly on a No. 6, coughing and giggling in equal measure.

Tunbridge Wells Grammar School for Girls was pretty much as you might imagine. Many hundreds of educated young ladies from a variety of backgrounds, all marshalled and directed by a group of mainly single women in their forties and fifties, some of whom were extraordinarily sweet and others storm troopers in tweed.

Our one well-known alumna was Virginia Wade, a famous tennis player who somehow got it together to win Wimbledon at one point. I would say she is a pretty typical ex-Tunbridge Wells girl. If you ever see her on telly, and she pops up from time to time to give her views on tennis, you will note that she is sweetly unfashionable and unerringly polite, in some ways a bit like a Victorian throwback. This, I think, is what the headmistress hoped we'd all turn out like.

Our headmistress was visually unthreatening, looking as she did like a twin-set-and-pearls type, but she had a rod of steel running through her and this was evident whenever there was any punishment to be meted out. I was a good girl, so it was unusual for me to see much of her, but she left fear in her wake, and a hushed respect coupled with terror would descend on everyone in the corridor should we spot her heading towards us.

I went back to the school recently for a speech day. It was a surreal experience. The new headmistress belonged to the twenty-first century, having as she did a normal hairstyle and normal clothes. We all sang the school song, which I had completely forgotten and have immediately suppressed, so I couldn't even tell you one line from it, but it was full of worthy sentiments, almost like a hymn, with nothing about smoking on the bus or pissing about during Latin in it.

The headmistress introduced me by saying something like: 'There are girls who are hugely academically gifted who apply themselves to their work, and there are others who mostly fly by the seat of their pants. Please welcome Jo Brand!' This didn't really chime with my memory of the place, as I did very well in my O-levels and didn't really get into trouble until I went to school in Hastings.

Among all the tweed and pudding-bowl haircuts, there was one cuckoo in the nest – our science teacher. She was a blonde siren, voluptuous and bursting out of her lab coat, and her appearance was the sort that promised untold delights to pervy middle-aged men. I thought sex lessons with her would be a hoot, but unfortunately she just did the 'insert the penis' mantra like all other science teachers and I was hugely disappointed.

My French teacher was like an elderly stick insect. She wore the most amazing bloomers I had ever seen in my life. They looked like they had been plucked from a Dickens novel, worn by someone like Betsey Trotwood, and they extended down to almost below her knees. How did we know? Because she would sit at the desk with her legs wide open and in between chanting, 'Je vais à la boulangerie' and 'Où est la gare?' and suchlike, many of us would deliberately drop pencils or rubbers on the floor so we could have a quick gander.

Bullying was not something, thankfully, that I experienced at this school, from other girls at least. If it was going on, I was blissfully unaware of it and pretty quickly I fell in with a group of warm, friendly girls who became close friends.

I liked sport generally. I didn't really have an athletic build, being slightly short, but I wasn't fat at that point and I could shift my arse when I had to. I liked netball particularly because it was a real team game in which you depended on others and I played wing attack which meant I got the opportunity to score fairly often. A sport I wasn't so keen on was hockey. Once you've been hit round the ankles a few times by some hulking great brute of a girl, it kind of loses its appeal. So at some point during my hockey career, I chose to be a goalkeeper. This was because you were togged up with loads of protection, like shin pads, you were the only player allowed to kick the ball as well as hit it with your stick and there were long periods of inactivity when you leaned against the goalpost. I would have had a fag if I could. I always remember hockey being played on muddy fields on cold, wet days, whereas it always seemed to be sunny when we were playing netball. False memory syndrome again, I suppose.

Some months after I arrived at Tunbridge Wells and having been allotted a place in the school netball team, I found our team playing against my old school which contained some girls who had been my friends. I'm ashamed to say that they seemed to me to have become country bumpkins, compared to the sophisticated Tunbridge Wells girls I was now spending my time with. It was a painful lesson to learn and it sent me the certain message that I had moved on from my old school and was now a grammar-school girl, much as I felt in my heart that this shouldn't be the case. All the awkward promises to stay in touch had melted away after a couple of months and it was as if we had never been close. So if any of those girls from Homewood are reading this, I apologise if I came across as a nobhead and I fully confess I was being one.

My best friend Paula came from a resolutely working-class Catholic background and had seven siblings and the most gloriously chaotic household you could imagine. After a while, as I was finding the journey a bit of a struggle, it was arranged that I would stay at

Paula's one or two nights a week and together we would stay at my Auntie Margie's one night a week. Auntie Margie was the mother of the baby, Elizabeth, that my brothers and I had dropped in a pond when we were younger, although she remained blissfully ignorant about the details at that point.

At Paula's, we slept three in a bed, the telly was on all the time, the noise level was at eleven most of the time and I absolutely loved it. Coming from a home in which my parents still tightly controlled our viewing habits, it was like being released into Wonderland a couple of nights a week.

School life quickly settled into the well-worn routine so beloved of children all over the world. I enjoyed school a lot, got on with everybody pretty well, behaved myself and did my work. I wouldn't say I was the star of the class, but I hovered in the top ten most of the time.

My favourite lesson was Latin, for some weird reason. I loved Caesar's *The Gallic Wars* and was really attracted to all these soldiers 'mounting the ramparts' and 'sending dispatches to Cicero'. There was something comforting about repeating endless declensions of nouns, or was it verbs? Can't remember but I loved it. What made all the difference was having the sweetest, most self-effacing teacher ever. The poor woman had been saddled with the name of Miss Polmounter, not a name you'd really want to go into teaching with. But because she was such a sweetie, we didn't use it against her because we were all so fond of her. Nothing much very exciting ever happened in Latin lessons apart from once, just after I'd had a BCG inoculation and the top of my arm had become a big, infected lump, tempting my friend Julia to give it a slightly too hard punch. My arm gently exploded, spewing pus all over my shirt, giving us something to talk about for weeks afterwards and leaving me with a very attractive scar that looks like a love bite.

Speaking of which, boys were starting to enter the frame round about the age of twelve or thirteen, although Tunbridge Wells Grammar School for Girls was the sort of school where teenage pregnancies were not so much frowned upon as met with histrionics, complete with screaming and tearing out of hair.

I remember my first kiss very well indeed. I think you'll find most girls do. It was at a party, and I suspect I was probably about twelve. I had hooked up with this slightly spotty young man whose name now escapes me. I didn't really fancy him very much but had decided that my first kiss was something to get over and done with, a bit like your first smear. He seemed as good a candidate as any. He was a bit of a shit dancer, but who isn't at that age? I think someone had smuggled some extremely weak beer in, so we all thought we were pissed out of our heads. And as the 'slowies' kicked off, I realised the moment was nigh. The face belonging to the boy in question loomed towards me and I shut my eyes and hoped for the best. To say it wasn't nice is underplaying the sheer horror of it all. A wet, slimy tongue pushed its way into my mouth and moved in a very unimaginative circular direction for what seemed like a thousand years. I was too surprised to respond in any constructive way apart from managing a quick poke in and out of my tongue now and again. Mercifully, it finally stopped and I pulled away feeling a mixture of revulsion at the practicalities of it and ecstasy at a developmental barrier finally hurdled. I think at that point, poor guy, I made my excuses, backed towards the door and headed off into the night, not wanting to repeat the experience until I was about seventy. Thankfully, I've met much better kissers since then but I could well understand how a crap first kiss could send you sprinting to a convent.

One thing I had mixed feelings about at school was athletics. I was in most of the teams – hockey, netball, tennis – but one thing I couldn't stand was athletics. I wasn't really built like an athlete, being less than willowy and a bit short. I'm not at all sure the sports teacher, a curious mixture of manly and horribly enthusiastic, was very keen on me. During an athletics session in the summer, she divided us all into fours to run the 400 metres and for some reason bunged me in with the three fastest runners in the school. I kept up with them for about the first seven metres and then they began to pull away, and as I saw their backs disappearing into the distance and became aware of the amused glances of the rest of the class, I realised I was going to get a right drubbing. By the time they had finished, I was only a third of the way round and was forced to slog on alone, the last 200 metres almost matching the humiliation of the violin debacle at my previous school.

It's hard to work out when you're a kid why certain teachers instantly don't like you. In psychotherapy this is known as 'negative transference' and, put at its simplest, it involves an instinctive hostile reaction to someone you've just met that you cannot explain, even if they seem like a perfectly nice person.

Although the games mistress wasn't my greatest fan, this was more of a problem with another teacher I had, who singled me out for some nasty treatment and indulged in what I believed was mild bullying. This, of course, was disguised under the cover of my supposed shortcomings, including the assertion that I had a speech impediment and therefore would never be able to pass any spoken exams. My 'speech impediment' amounted to a very slight hiss when I pronounced the letter 's', and no one else had ever noted or commented on it.

I certainly wasn't aware of it, and neither were any of my family. I always thought teachers were supposed to help prevent bullying, not be the bullies themselves. Still, I suppose it was a good lesson: that occasionally in life – or for some poor sods more frequently than that – people will take an instant dislike to you and make your life a misery for no reason. Initially I kept quiet about the handful of instances when this teacher singled me out and made me look like a fool, because I was embarrassed about it and thought it was my fault. We all want to be liked and, I suppose, we all assume that if we are nice and polite to people there is no reason for them to go on the offensive. But things got steadily worse. This teacher would show me up in front of the class and try to make the other girls laugh at me.

These frequent, humiliating allusions to my general crapness were accompanied by a fair amount of sarcasm and it got to the stage where I was reluctant to be in this teacher's class, or indeed go to school at all.

So, I eventually mentioned this to my mum, who I suppose was shocked to find out that in what she had assumed was a middle-class environment populated by sensible teachers, this horrible person had it in for her little girl. And my mum cannot abide bullying of any sort; it makes her angrier than anything else. She is someone who, when she is angry, does revenge big time and will not put up with any kind of injustice. So ...

My mother, with all guns blazing, headed up to the school to 'sort it out', and if there's one thing my mum is good at it's giving someone a general sort-out. It seemed that almost instantly the problem melted away and I had no more grief at all. If only I could keep my mum in a cupboard and get her to sort out all the negative things in my life.

Other highlights and lowlights of life at school were as follows:

- A friend of mine managing to insert a tampon during our geography O-level exam. I won't tell you her name – I'm sure you'll understand why.

What was particularly impressive about this incident was the fact that it was during an exam, when teachers watch you like a hawk for fear of any cheating going on. Our teachers would not only sit at the front with a beady eye on all of us, from time to time they would stroll up and down the aisles of the big school hall, leaning over us and doing big, long, hard stares at our work. So all power to her for managing what would have involved a fair bit of shuffling around. It was the talk of our little group of friends for ages afterwards.

- Winning a prize in the fifth year and being permitted to choose a book. I asked for an anthology of Bob Dylan lyrics and had to wrestle with the headmistress who thought it was a highly inappropriate book for a grammar-school girl to be reading. A friend of mine who allowed the school to choose her book for her ended up with a volume on polishing pebbles, guaranteed to make you lose consciousness at the first page. In retrospect, I made a wise decision.

- Finding ever new and resourceful ways of getting out of having a communal shower every week. Even though I wasn't overweight, the idea filled me with absolute horror. Having been forced into the shower once, I vowed that I would never go in there again. I never did.

This meant that I had to come up with a truly impressive list of excuses and these included:

1. 'I've got my period.'
This excuse was a good one, because obviously in a class of thirty or so girls, the teachers did not have a chart of everyone's menstrual cycles, so you could get away with at least two periods a month.

2. 'I've got a cold.'
This was a dodgy one, because the more gung-ho teachers would say something like 'Well, having a shower will be good for you.' So I had to make sure I only used this if a weedy, sympathetic teacher was on shower duty.

3. Once, when I'd exhausted numbers 1 and 2, I just started to cry for no reason and pretended I had problems at home. This worked a treat, but could only be used once in case they got suspicious and contacted my parents.

- A girl in our class turning up for school one day looking as if she had been tarred and feathered. Her little brother had cut off all her gorgeous, long, white-blond hair while she was asleep and although it had distressed the poor girl enormously, it was hard not to laugh.

- Piano lessons with my piano teacher, Miss Funnell (yes, that was her name), who took a somewhat hardline approach to scales and would threaten to whack me on the hand with the thin edge of a ruler if I bolloxed them up. This did not encourage me to get them right, however.

Piano lessons became quite an ordeal in some ways. I was not good at practising, despite the fact that I knew she would come down hard on me if I wasn't up to scratch. So I found myself in the situation of being scared I might be rapped pretty much every week, and this made me not want to play the piano any more. I begged my parents to let me stop and they dug their heels in for a bit until they realised I was very unhappy. I never really told them why.

So, I liked school. I worked hard, I did OK academic-ally and I had really great friends whom I could have a laugh with. There had been whispers that I would do well enough to try for a place at Oxford or Cambridge, and all seemed set fair for a golden few years.

And then everything changed . . .

Chapter 7

Teenage Kicks

Towards the end of my fifth year, my parents, owing to my dad's job, decided to move to Hastings in Sussex. It wasn't that far from Tunbridge Wells, so I naturally assumed I would continue at the same school and was looking forward to swanning around the sixth-form common room, not having to wear uniform and sailing towards a posh-gob existence at Oxford or Cambridge.

This was not my own idea but one that had been instilled into me by the school, which got a fair few pupils into those august institutions every year. They were always portrayed as the ultimate Valhalla to aspire to, and I didn't really think seriously about whether I wanted to go there or not, I just assumed I would. This, of course, was encouraged by my mum and dad to a certain extent, as it would have been a great coup for a child of theirs to force her way in through the exclusive portals of what was still pretty much the preserve of the rich and upper classes.

Had my parents had any idea of what was about to happen, they would have happily made any arrangements necessary for me to stay on in Tunbridge Wells, but of course they didn't, and with me grumpily in tow, trying every trick in the book to be allowed to stay at the same school, they willingly jumped off the precipice of the status quo into a hellhole of appalling teenage behaviour which would test them to the limits of their sanity and beyond.

The main reason I didn't want to leave Tunbridge Wells was not particularly the school and the teachers, but more the fact that I was very comfortable with the group of friends that I had made and the life I had there. I was, and still am, quite a shy person and I have a horror of rooms full of people I don't know.

This may, of course, raise a question: 'Well, what on earth did you become a bloody stand-up comedian for, you dozy cow?' It's a fair question and I suppose the only answer I can give is this one.

First of all, I feel that it's not me up on stage, it's

someone else, a version of me, a confident, cleverer, funnier version of me. Added to that, as a comic clutching your mic, you are allotted some natural authority when you step on stage. You don't always retain it, but you've got it to start off with and that gives you some sense of power.

So, to me, the thought of having to make friends with an entirely new group of people filled me with trepidation.

My mother has always been an immovable object when she makes up her mind about something and although I'm pretty similar, I've never been able to match her for stubbornness. I suppose some of my bad behaviour as a teenager was an attempt to lock horns with my parents who, up until that point, had always had the final word.

I started as a pupil at Hastings High School for Girls and decided I wasn't going to like it. In fact, there were quite a few things not to like about it, one being that some of the teachers were more like characters out of a Dickens novel. One particular teacher, a strange-looking character, had not ended up teaching girls by accident. His personality had two overriding facets to it: grumpiness and perviness. So he would constantly berate us for our shortcomings on the homework front, while simultaneously making completely inappropriate comments about our chests, bums or any other areas he deemed were worth slavering over.

Having a feminist mother (not that she called herself that at the time), I was enormously resentful of any man who divided up women into a series of bits to be assessed and pronounced upon, and found myself getting very angry in his presence, to the point of occasionally nearly losing my temper. But I was a sixteen-year-old schoolgirl and he was a man with the gift of a whiplash tongue that vomited out sarcasm and bile at every given opportunity, and I guess I was just too scared to take him on.

Subconsciously, I think I had decided at that point that I wasn't going to fit into that school, so I gravitated towards the bad girls in my class and eventually found myself turning up for the register and then on a fairly regular basis leaving school in the car of a friend and going to a cafe on the seafront where we would spend most of the day smoking and eking out our meagre coins on one or two coffees.

I suppose I bunked off because I never really had any emotional investment in the place. I didn't particularly like the big, square, modern, ugly block, probably built in the sixties. It would have given Prince Charles a few shivers down the spine, had he ever had the chance to assess the building.

As far as schoolwork was concerned, I knew I was bright enough to hold my own and I hovered around the middle of the class, occasionally slumping towards the bottom. But I didn't give a toss. The resentment I felt about having been uprooted fuelled my bad behaviour. I didn't make any effort to get to know the teachers and gave no thought whatsoever to my future in terms of university and work.

Our skiving sessions were pretty uneventful. We went to the same cafe on the seafront most days and if we did do something different it usually involved mooching round the shops, although this didn't happen very often, as we were worried we might be spotted by a teacher.

I can really hardly remember a thing about the academic stuff I did at that school. I chose to take French, German, English and Sociology A-levels, although I dropped German after a short while because it was too much. I'd like to think I wasn't the worst pupil, as someone in our class actually called *Wuthering Heights* 'Withering Huts' on an exam paper.

Sport was a bit of a disaster at this school. I had given up all thoughts of running and jumping due to the humiliation at the hands of the sports teacher at my old school, but I was quite good at throwing things, hence I was chosen to chuck the javelin on sports day.

When that day arrived, as was our habit, several of us disappeared into the toilets to have a quick smoke before the activities began. I pulled out my sad little packet of No. 6 and a box of Swan Vesta, lit the little cigarette and, mindful of not leaving matches lying around, blew the match out and put it back in the box. The problem was that I hadn't blown the match out properly and when it was deposited in a full box of its companions, the whole bloody box blew up in my hand. Yes, it hurt. It left a huge, blackish-brownish burn on my hand that was really painful. Realising it would not be an easy injury to explain to a first-aid person, I ran cold water over it and wrapped it in a paper towel.

This, of course, meant that throwing the javelin with my right hand, now covered with a huge, weeping burn, wasn't going to happen, so I went on to the field in the rather ridiculous position of having to throw the javelin with my left hand. Well, of course, it went about three feet, well below the expectations of the watching crowd, completing my general humiliation in the entire range of sports, from running to throwing.

That was the only occasion I think that smoking

directly affected my life in an acutely negative way. I had been smoking on and off since I first started taking the school bus to Tunbridge Wells. I remember one of the older kids on the bus had a packet and offered me one, the equivalent of a heroin dealer for school kids. I had always loved the smell of cigarettes. Both my grandma and granddad smoked moderately. Of course, the first puff of a fag makes you realise that they don't taste like they smell, but even though I didn't really enjoy it and ending up putting it out after only a few puffs, I ridiculously persevered, probably because my parents were so anti it and part of me wanted to have my own secret little world that had nothing to do with them.

I would either buy or get someone older to buy ten No. 6 (the common-as-muck fags) from about the age of thirteen and we would smoke them on the bus, blowing the smoke out of the window of the top deck and feeling very pleased with ourselves. When I stayed at my friend Paula's, in Tunbridge Wells, her mum smoked and we would occasionally nick one of her Benson & Hedges, which we thought were remarkably posh, and blow the smoke out of the bedroom window. I'm sure her mum must have noticed the smell, but she never said anything.

When I got older and was in control of my own destiny and cigarette intake, I chose Rothmans. I've no idea why. I remember an ad for them at the time which showed a pilot's arm at the controls of a plane. The byline was something like: 'For the man who is in control.' No mention of a woman, but I'm sure I subconsciously absorbed the message about being in control.

For maximum sophistication, I would smoke either St Moritz, the menthol cigarettes that had a gold band round them, or Sobranie Cocktails, which were multi-coloured and which we thought made us look interesting, although I'm sure they made us look like pathetic teenagers who wanted to look interesting. The great anti-smoking wave of terror didn't really hit until the late eighties and early nineties, so you could pretty much smoke everywhere – on planes, in hospitals, in shops and on buses. I think they drew the line at lighting up in church, but I had turned away from all that by then, so I wasn't too bothered.

Squash was another sport I played at school and, much to my surprise, I became rather good at it (the obvious joke that I squashed people has been made many times over the years). I became school squash champion, perhaps the only tangible success I managed while I was there.

What I loved about squash was that you could hit the ball really hard – it was so satisfying. It's also rather a sneaky tactical game where you often get the chance to plop the ball gently off a very low part of the wall, thus forcing a rhino-like charge from your opponent all the way across the court to try to return it. On the odd occasion they don't manage to stop in time and that's very entertaining. In fact, one of my opponents once knocked out two of his front teeth attempting to return a ball. I felt guilty for weeks.

I remember the girl I played in the final was big and tough but surprisingly nimble on her feet. I think at that time I was about nine stone, so I had the advantage of manoeuvrability. Still, it was a bitterly hard-fought contest. I realised she was getting knackered, so I made her run a lot and eventually I think the poor girl was so exhausted that she just caved in. I don't know if I even told my parents of my victory. I was no longer seeking their approval or wanting pats on the head from them. It was a bit sad really, but in my mind I rationalised it by convincing myself that they had started it and it was all their fault.

Life moved on, days were spent in the cafe on the seafront and I gently seethed at home, feeling hard done by that I had been taken away from a school I really loved. I spent a lot of time in my bedroom, reading, writing crap poetry and trying to make the words of the great songwriters fit my life and experience: not easy when most of them were American blokes. I was very resentful and this manifested in as much rebellion as I could manage at home – not a lot because my dad was quite intimidating. Of course, parents keep things from you and I wasn't aware of how low my father was feeling. He just seemed self-centred and I was wary of his bad temper.

My brother Bill, who was also finding life difficult, took a different tack and just retreated inside himself. He never said much, never smiled and wandered about very quietly as if to say, 'I don't want to get involved.' And who could blame him?

During my first year in the sixth form, while I was still doing German, a German exchange was arranged for those of us attempting A-level. Partners in that far-off land were randomly picked and I ended up with a strapping, rosy-cheeked, extraordinarily unfashionable girl called Bettina who favoured bright-yellow miniskirts, knee-length white socks and prissy little blouses, an ensemble that made her look about ten, except for the fact that her arse was on show.

The whole experience was an ordeal. The family

consisted of Bettina, her parents and a rather frightening looking older brother whom I kept well away from. On my first day there we celebrated with a glass of something that tasted like burned old tyres. I'm not really sure what it was but I assume it was whisky-based. I was there for a couple of weeks and it just so happened that Hitler's birthday fell in that period. Much to my surprise, the family informed me in words I barely understood that we were going out to celebrate. We ended up in some kind of pub with a few blokes wandering around in lederhosen and a lot of singing of God knows what sort of songs going on. I was on *sieg heil* alert, but thankfully it didn't go that far and after what seemed like twelve hours of back-slapping and 'Tomorrow Belongs To Me' renditions we finally headed home. I felt like a true outsider, although I gritted my teeth, smiled and tried not to say anything.

I have never held anything against the Germans, however, like some people. Some years into my comedy career, I wrote a column in the *Independent* which was syndicated to the *Mirror*, of which Piers Morgan was editor at the time. During Euro 96, England were playing Germany in the semi-final and Paul Gascoigne was depicted on the front page with a German helmet on his head, accompanied by the word '*Achtung*'.

I felt this was just too much anti-German sentiment, particularly as my brother had married a German woman and she had expressed some anxiety about coming over to this country because of it. This was real and not imagined, as some lads had taken to vandalising German makes of car. Their actions were almost completely mindless, but not quite because at least they had learned the difference between foreign cars and British ones.

So I resigned my column in a pathetic sort of protest and subsequently found out over the years that Mr Morgan was unhappy about my resignation. I know this because every time I was in a room with him, be it a green room or a TV studio, he went on and on about it to the assembled crowd. He has since apologised to me. I've no idea why. I was surprised because I wasn't a particularly important person to him. I couldn't give him a job, couldn't advance his career. Perhaps he thinks I'm a really wonderful person. Who knows?

Incidentally, while I was in Germany, I was out for a walk on my own and I came across a group of children aged about nine or ten, maybe six or seven of them, actually stoning another child, who was standing completely still and crying. I abhor bullying of any sort and I regret that the compulsion to indulge in it seems to be an essential part of the psyche of many individuals, men and women alike. As I had, despite hours of German lessons, a pretty poor grasp of the language, I hesitated briefly, worrying that they would laugh at me. But the poor little fellow was so distressed, I waded in, shouting in English at them and managing to look fierce enough to scatter them. The problem was, once I'd involved myself, I didn't know what to do next. I suppose I gave the child a chance to leg it, but my German wasn't really up to 'Are you all right? Do you want me to take you home? Where do you live?' I walked on, thinking cynically that as soon as I had disappeared over the horizon they would probably resume their horrible actions.

I've had a few strange encounters with Germans. On holiday in Malta with a friend once, we arrived back at our hotel slightly pissed to find a group of very drunk Germans in the bar, that you had to pass by to get to the lifts. As we walked past, there was laughter and I caught the word '*dicke*' which means fat. I was not massive at that time, but not thin either, and having had a few drinks, I felt quite up for a fight. Having a brother married to a German was handy, as I'd picked up a few German phrases, such as 'Fuck off' ('*Verpiss dich*' in case you're interested), so I stalked over, my courage completely drink-fuelled, and threw out the few paltry phrases I knew. The Germans were a combination of amused and shocked and I didn't hang around to soak up any further reactions – we disappeared into the lift as fast as our slightly drunken legs would carry us.

The next morning I decided to get up for an early swim. I don't subscribe to all that 'towels by the pool' nonsense when it comes to Germans, although there were a few members of the group I had berated the night before laid out by the pool, and it really felt like running the gauntlet getting past them. However, I held my head high and marched past as snootily as I could manage and selected a deckchair right at the other end of the pool. I was mightily relieved as my bum headed towards it, until it actually made contact. There was a deafening ripping noise and I continued to descend through the material until my arse made contact with the ground and I found myself sitting in the deckchair rather than on it. The horror. Naturally this scene had been witnessed by the group of Germans who had been my tormentors the previous night. Oh how they laughed, pointed and scrabbled for their cameras. I extracted myself with as much dignity as I could and fled. And I still like Germans.

Bettina's stay with us on the return part of the exchange was even worse in some ways. She was a pleasant enough person, but our inability to communicate on anything except a very basic level didn't make it easy for us to have a laugh. I tried not to hold it against her that her parents were out-of-the-closet Nazis, but we did run into some problems. It was nigh impossible to get her to eat anything. She turned her nose up at a whole gamut of English dishes that my mum half desperately, half grumpily placed in front of her and resolutely refused to eat even baked beans, our national dish. What an insult to our culinary skills! It was a difficult few weeks and as the end loomed, I looked towards it with relief.

On Bettina's last night I planned to take her to Hastings Pier for an evening out, as there was a band on. Having arranged to meet friends there whom I knew would laugh at poor Bettina's sartorial choices, I offered a makeover and a loan of some of my clothes. At that time I was heavily into the hippy side of things, having dallied briefly with skinhead fashion (tonic suit and monkey boots) at my old school. Consequently, I could be found wearing Loon jeans (highly flared cotton ones in a variety of acid-bright colours) and cotton T-shirts with drawstring sleeves. I also eschewed bras, despite the fact that my lovely friend Halcyon's mum, every time I went round there, tried to pin me down and put one on me with portentous warnings about my chest ending up near my shins in the not-too-distant future.

Halcyon was a good person who looked like a good person. She had beautiful blond hair and a very smiley face and there was not an ounce of malice in her. Her lovely family, consisting of lots of kids and a warm, cuddly mum, was a really comfortable group of people to spend time with. Halcyon went on to work in the caring professions, which I knew she would. My other main friend, Helen, from an Irish family, was laidback, warm and really good fun. We spent hours in her bedroom listening to David Bowie albums, trying on clothes and talking bollocks and an equal amount of time parading around town in our finest seventies garb, looking for excitement.

If required to posh up I could run to a Laura Ashley patterned skirt and glittery top (sounds hideous, doesn't it?). The effect was completed with a slosh of patchouli oil so strong it could repel local dogs from a distance of half a mile. So I dressed Bettina like me and did her hair and make-up. I took out the farm-girl pigtails and coaxed her into some more subtle make-up, used as she was to great slabs of bright-blue across her eyelids.

I was looking forward to the night, as there was a boy going who I really fancied. Can't even remember his name now, but we shall call him Rob. We set off excitedly and met a group of others by the pier, with my friends marvelling at the transformation of Bettina from horse-in-drag to passable beauty. The evening went well, we bopped about, had a few illegal drinks and then I looked over to the corner to see Bettina and Rob dancing together and snogging. And I still like Germans.

I think every girl has at least one psychotic episode of love in her career as a teenager, the more unsuitable the bloke, the better. And it is a strange mix of the most exquisite torture and glorious abandon, the balance, of course, being affected by how unrequited it is. Poetry, music, lying on your bed staring at the ceiling, having butterflies, crying, looking at yourself in the mirror wondering if you're ugly, waiting for the phone to ring, going for walks, staring out of the window, swearing at them and hating them fairly often, writing their name on everything, phoning them up and putting the phone down, writing letters and then tearing them up – these are all part of the unbearable, obsessive, ridiculous experience of 'lurve' as a teenager.

Hastings was full of foreign students and for one idyllic summer my heart was given to a lovely Italian boy called Claudio, who was dark-haired, dark-eyed and very cheeky. It was all pretty innocent – of a holding hands and snogging nature – and we were frequently accompanied by his not-quite-so-attractive friend, a role I was used to playing, who was enormously entertaining and whose party piece was a spectacular rendering of Winston Churchill's 'We will fight them on the beaches' speech, particularly appropriate for Hastings, as the local lads resented this influx of exotic maleness and were very threatened by it, to the point of encouraging big rucks on the seafront.

These so-called fights were really just an opportunity to work off some testosterone. Lots of eyeing-up would go on, followed by a bit of flailing around with fists. Thankfully, serious injury wasn't often a feature, but territorial feelings ran high and peppering them with a touch of xenophobia occasionally resulted in the cartoonish sight of a lot of grappling and quite a bit of falling over.

Claudio melted away at the end of the summer. We wrote fervently to each other and at Christmas a present arrived from him, an expression of his undying affection. It was a chain belt, probably the major fashion item of the time ... and it was utterly revolting. In the time-honoured custom of the fragile teenage romance, it completely put me off him. Our letters gradually dried up and I looked for joy nearer to home. The belt left home and went to take up residence in a charity shop.

I went on a date with a strangely nerdy young man whom I had met at the pier one night. He was a lovely, shy, bespectacled boy, who turned out to be an even worse kisser than the first one of my life. We met at a pub and after enduring two bouts of this unpleasantness, which was reminiscent of receiving mouth-to-mouth from an old bloke without teeth, I decided I had to do something drastic. Telling him I had to go to the toilet, I headed out of the door, went for a wee and plotted my escape route. There was a corridor leading from the toilets to outside, but it meant passing the door to the bar he was in, which had a pane of glass which started at waist height. So I got down on my hands and knees and proceeded gingerly towards freedom. As I was passing the door, I looked up to check I was not being observed and there was my beau looking down at me, arms folded, with a half tragic, half furious look on his face. Much as I felt guilty, I could not bear to have to give an explanation, so I rose to my feet and ran for it. Haven't seen him since.

During this period, having a mother who was a social worker had its pros and cons. My mum had been training for the job since I was about nine or ten, when she began a course at a local college. There wasn't a huge change in my life, we still saw her a lot. However, she would be on call several nights a month and I have a very strong memory of her one night, all done up in a posh dress, ready to go out to what they called a 'dinner and dance' in those days, and having to divert and go and section someone under the Mental Health Act. I suspect many social workers and doctors turn up for these things in an interesting variety of clothes.

I think my dad found my mum's new career quite difficult, and it caused tension between them. They were very careful not to let this spill over into our family life, but as a kid, when you know your parents so well, atmospheres are very easy to pick up. All us kids were aware that things weren't going well. Snatches of arguments could be heard at night when we were in bed, and we all knew that things were very strained between them.

Because of my mother's social work, I felt it incumbent upon me to do vaguely defined 'good works'. So Halcyon and I signed up to spend a week in a stately home in Cheshire, caring for adults who were severely physically and mentally disabled, to give their carers a break. I suppose my motives were to do with having had it instilled in us from an early age that we were very lucky to be who we were and that many other people were not so fortunate. For a while, my mum was attached to a psychiatric hospital and we would go there to play badminton when I was a teenager. There would be several patients wandering about in the grounds and I never felt scared in the way you were meant to. So I was happy to get involved with those with learning disabilities, totally different as they are from mental health problems. Also, in my selfish way, I thought we would have a good laugh and get pissed quite a lot.

This trip opened my eyes to the harshness of the world in more ways than one. It was very exciting to be living in what effectively was a huge mansion, specifically converted for the purpose, but it was also weird to be forced to spend time with people whom you'd only just met. We, the carers, were a mixed bunch – men and women of all ages – and we all got on pretty well apart from one man who had rather a strange manner. He was slightly over-friendly and a bit too touchy for my liking. He would always invade my personal space, put his face too close to mine, put his arm round me or run his hand down my back in a completely over-familiar way. All of this made me feel most uncomfortable and a little bit intimidated by him. Time has mercifully erased his name from my mind.

Our day consisted of washing, bathing and feeding our group, interspersed with visits to local attractions. In the evenings, after a long, hard day, we would all repair to the pub and get pissed. One night my companions were all knackered and wanted to go home, but I was up for a bit of a lock-in. I'd met a group of people who were mostly teenage locals. We'd sat near them and all got chatting. They were very friendly and a good laugh and I felt at ease with them, with the help of a few bottles of lager obviously.

So I waved my colleagues away, saying I'd find a lift home on my own. They were dubious, but I assured them I'd be fine and continued drinking. When the pub eventually closed, a squaddie who'd been hanging round the fringes of the group said he was going past where I was staying and he'd drop me off. Alcohol had blunted my personal-safety antennae, as it does, and I gratefully accepted. We got in his car, chatted happily together and as we came up to the rather grand gates of where I was staying, I pointed and said, 'That's it there.'

He replied, 'I know,' and drove straight past it and on down the main road. Suddenly all the horror films I had seen started to play in my head. The cliché about being paralysed in these situations is absolutely true and the sheer, overwhelming panic cuts through the alcohol-induced blanket of smugness. Very soon after, he turned off down a little unlit lane, drove about two hundred yards, stopped the car and turned towards me. I seriously thought I was going to be raped or worse and so something inside me made me go on the offensive and I screamed at him, 'What the fuck do you think you're going to do now?'

To my enormous surprise and relief, he put his head in his hands and began to cry, eventually explaining that he was lonely, missed his fiancée and could he just take me back home? Of course he could. Of such incidents are comedy routines constructed.

We pulled up outside the house and as I got out of the car, he asked me if he could take me to dinner the following night. Yet again, I ran. It would have been bad enough if this had been the only traumatic incident on this volunteer holiday, but more was to come.

After an enjoyable but hard week, we arrived at the final night. The group we were looking after had gone home and we were all staying that night and leaving in the morning. Of course, a party was suggested, drink was purchased and after a lot more drinking someone suggested the house, which was enormous, would be a good one to play sardines in. The lights were turned off and we scattered to hide in different rooms, the hazy rules dictating that people who found others had to hide with them. I found a quiet corner in a little room at the end of the corridor and lay behind a chair, feeling half excited, half terrified, as I'm not a fan of the dark.

As kids, we always had a nightlight in the room, the implication being that the dark is not a good thing, although this may be for practical reasons – you bump into things. I think I just had a rabid imagination and took slightly too seriously those stories about bogeymen. I also remember my mum talking about the film *Psycho* and how much it had frightened her, and that played on my mind when I was a kid.

For a while, I lived in a cottage in Shropshire. It was unusual for me to be there on my own and one windy, dark night I couldn't sleep. It was about two in the morning and suddenly someone started knocking on the door. My heart nearly came out of my mouth. I tried hiding under the duvet but the knocking continued and in my head some mad, murdering type had made his way to my door and was waiting outside with a machete. But I couldn't just lie there and do nothing, so I made my way to the door and stood there as the faint knocking continued. Eventually I couldn't stand it any longer and opened the door. There was no one there, the wind was causing the knocker to gently tap on the door. I stayed up the rest of that night with the bread knife next to me.

Back to sardines. After a few minutes, I heard someone outside the door of the little room I was hiding in and, assuming it was one of the boys I was good friends with, I started to laugh. My laugh was answered with scary maniacal laughter and this thing burst into the room, screaming and hooting. I was terrified and ran for the door, hitting a low coffee table that had been obscured by the dark. I landed on top of it, breaking it and the thing landed on top of me, tearing at my clothes and slobbering on my neck.

I screamed my bloody head off. Nothing happened for what seemed like ages, then eventually I heard shouts and the lights were turned on to reveal that Mr Slightly Pervy Man was my attacker. I was crying and accusing him, but he somehow managed to convince everyone that he was only having a laugh and got a bit carried away and I was hysterical.

So we decided to call it a day, I was taken off to the kitchen for a cup of cocoa and a calm-down and Mr S.P.M. was sent off.

As it was late, I set off for bed and started to get undressed in my room, still slightly shocked and upset. Out of the corner of my eye, I saw the curtains move and did that weird thing of saying in a croaky voice, 'Who's there?' like they're going to say, ''Tis I, Mr Slightly Pervy Man.' For, indeed, it was he, there for round two. I screeched at the top of my voice and people appeared within seconds.

Mr Slightly Pervy Man was offered the choice of speaking to the police or pissing off straight away. Unsurprisingly, he chose the latter and I was left to ruminate on some valuable if unpalatable lessons learned.

Chapter 8

An Education in Skiving

My first year at my new school had not been very auspicious. I hadn't spent long actually in the place and I hadn't really done very much work apart from just enough to keep my head above water. Days were spent in work avoidance and dallying around on the seafront enjoying myself.

The seafront had a lot to offer the out-of-control teenager. There were loads of pubs, there was the pier and there were many cafes to hang out in. Much of my time, if the weather was good enough, was spent just sitting on the beach. I could normally find some co-conspirators from school to join me. The main ones were Helen, Lucy and Mouse, and there were two girls

I'd met who didn't go to our school called Barb and Hattie. Everyone looked like a hippie and there were long skirts and bare feet everywhere.

My parents used to go mad about the bare feet thing. Yes, I suppose they were right about all the stuff on the pavements. They weren't exactly surfaces you could eat your dinner off, covered as they were with every imaginable substance ranging from ice cream to dog shit to chewing gum. I didn't care though. It was a mark of honour to have filthy feet, and they became so toughened that it was easy to walk on the hard, pebbly beach and give my feet the occasional rinse in the sea.

Although there were arcades on the pier, we didn't spend much time in them, mainly due to lack of money. Pretty much the only time we went to the pier would be to see bands playing. I've never been a fan of fruit machines because I know they are going to swallow everything you own in the end, despite the false hope they give you along the way.

When I was still at school, my friend Helen and I got a job as cleaners in a TB hospital. Oh the romance. We would do Sunday mornings from seven till about one. We wore charming overalls and caps over our hair, as we had to be very aware of the possibility of infection. The job consisted mainly of hoovering, mopping floors and what cleaners call 'damp dusting' round the wards. The wards were full of elderly, grey-looking people whom I felt immensely sorry for. We would try to get a break as often as we could and go out by the bins for a fag. Perhaps the aspect of the job that I found most difficult to deal with was emptying buckets of scraps into the deliciously named 'pig bin'. This was a massive metal bin out in the yard, filled with all the food scraps from the week before, so you can imagine what it smelled like. I would find it very difficult to lean over it in order to pour the contents of the bucket in without gagging.

We always used to do one little cosmetic task for ourselves every week, and that was sorting out what I called 'smoker's finger' – that is, dealing with the attractive yellow staining that the holding of a fag does to your hands. Helen would fill two mugs with warm water and put a tiny bit of bleach in and we would stand in the kitchen with our two fag-holding fingers dipped in the cup for about five minutes. Worked a treat.

At the end of our shift we would always get a Sunday lunch, and then I would go home and have one there too. I'm sure that didn't help my attempts to maintain a lovely, svelte figure.

When I was about sixteen, I also had a Saturday morning job in Boots to give me some spending money for going out. It was good fun. I worked on the till, but was occasionally moved to the make-up counter, where, for some reason, lots of women would come and ask my advice about shades of eye shadow and lipstick and what would suit their colouring. Well, I knew bog all about make-up, but I got stuck in with gusto, offering my uninformed advice, and it seemed to send most women away happy.

When I was on the till, a few shamefaced boys would line up with packets of condoms, and some were so embarrassed they wouldn't even make it to the front of the queue. I felt so sorry for them. At least they were buying condoms and not leaving it up to the woman. I've always wondered if, apart from machines in toilets, there could be some other way for teenage boys to get their hands on condoms without having to face the amused look of a shop assistant. It's hard enough getting boys to use them anyway, we shouldn't put obstacles in their path.

It was at Boots that I first set eyes on a man who was to become a rather powerful influence in my life.

At this point, I was struggling against my parents' rigid sense of what I should be and where my life should go. I think my parents judged me by their own generational standards, so that they expected me to reap the benefits of the hard work they put in to haul themselves up from very working-class roots to arrive somewhere in the lower-middle classes. This meant that I was expected to go to university and end up with a profession. Therefore, anything that happened in my life that seemed to demonstrate that I would become a bit of a no-hoper made them very anxious. It seemed impossible to explain to them that underneath I was an OK person and wasn't going to dive headfirst into drugs or marry a serial killer. The gulf between us was just too wide.

They didn't like my friends much because, to them, they were sirens tempting me into venues where sex and drugs were available on tap, and I got the feeling they longed for the days when a clergyman's daughter was my best friend and my worst misdemeanour was being late for bell-ringing practice.

Actually, my friends weren't that bad, it's just that their parents were more liberal, so I suppose it seemed to my mum and dad that their daughters were on the loose and dangerous. It was all to do with expectations. Everyone I knew was experimenting with drink and drugs, but, ironically, most of them did it in quite a sensible way.

Helen, Lucy and Mouse all came from nice families and just happened to be allowed out more than I was – that was all there was to it. I'm sure my mum and dad thought they were going to all-night sex parties flowing with cocaine. If only Hastings had been that exciting.

My parents lagged behind those of my friends in terms of what I was allowed to do. If my friends were allowed out until eleven, I was allowed out until ten. If my friends were allowed to go to a party and stay the night, I had to be picked up by my dad in his pyjamas and dressing gown. At the age of sixteen or seventeen, being prevented from truly being part of one's peer group is probably the greatest humiliation one can suffer. I begged, I cajoled, I ranted, but there were so many occasions on which they stood their ground and refused to give in. My dad was going through a bad time, suffering a quite serious depression, which meant he had a very short fuse, and on numerous occasions I pushed him too far.

The problem was I didn't realise my dad had depression at the time and so I didn't take it into account in my dealings with him. I was fed up myself. The average person doesn't know a great deal about depression. All of us say, 'I'm really depressed' from time to time, if we've got too much work, or our football team hasn't done well in the league (Crystal Palace, seeing as you asked) but these, usually fleeting, periods of misery are not what psychiatrists mean by depression.

As a nurse, I encountered the two types of depression that psychiatrists are faced with treating: reactive depression and endogenous depression. Reactive depression is pretty much what it sounds like: a depression that arises as a reaction to a life event, be it bereavement, a relationship breaking up or something along those lines. On the other hand, an endogenous depression is something that comes from inside you, cannot be explained by outside forces and seems to be caused by a biochemical imbalance in the brain. Of course, the situation is more complex than that, but, put simply, these are the two types.

And depression can be so serious for some people that it can virtually paralyse them. Extremely depressed people can hardly move, they are so gripped by it. On the whole, and again I am generalising, endogenous depression has a far greater physical effect on the body. It affects sleep, and particularly results in people waking early in the morning, and it affects the amount you eat – many very depressed people stop eating altogether. Everything about the person slows down.

As far as my dad was concerned, it was difficult for me to see that anything was going on with him. I just assumed he was angry a lot of the time because I was misbehaving. On the whole, I tiptoed around him, but there were times when we would have big rows about how loud I was playing my music or what time I got home after a night out. On the odd occasion, things would escalate and rather than stepping back from the fight and trying to be co-operative and calm, I would lose my temper and answer back. At these times, my dad would lose his temper too and lash out at me. I'm sure he doesn't remember much of this and regrets what he does remember enormously, but it resulted in me being frightened of him most of the time.

So to me, his depression was characterised by grumpiness and occasional aggression, but for him I'm sure it was much worse. Many writers – and they say eighty per cent of writers have suffered from some sort of depression at one time or another – have tried to describe depression. Churchill famously characterised it as 'the black dog', for example. From my experience, it seems that some huge, dark blanket wraps itself around you, making you feel sad, angry and hopeless and preventing all normal interaction with the rest of society. There are sometimes elements of anxiety and paranoia, and many people become suicidal. Eventually, my dad sought help and was prescribed anti-depressants, and I think they changed his life. The fact that drugs do change things would indicate that there is a huge biochemical element to this kind of depression. These days, he is a different person – more relaxed, hopeful and content.

I spent many evenings sitting miserably in my bedroom listening to Bob Dylan and Neil Young as a series of boys called to try to persuade me to go out. I'm making it sound like there was a never-ending stream of suitors. There wasn't, but there were enough to make me realise I wasn't the female equivalent of the Elephant Man. And they were all very different. A blond, bearded hippy with John Lennon glasses called Cat or Dog or Tiger, a more down-to-earth, curly-haired, denim-clad colossus who worked in a garage and the odd friend of my brother from school.

And then there was Dave.

As far as my parents were concerned, I looked wrong, I behaved wrong and I wasn't the respectable young lady heading for great things that they had hoped for. If I had asked my mum and dad what sort of boyfriend they would least like me to become involved with, I suspect they would have said an arrogant, disobedient, non-committed and (with their working-class roots) posh boy.

Unfortunately for them, Dave was all these things. When I first saw him he was the perfect seventies representation of a boy. Skinny as a rake, tall, masses of long, curly hair, very posh voice and a sense of adventurousness about him that I hadn't really come across before. He drifted in and out of my radar for a while. I would see him disappearing out of a pub as I walked in, I spotted him at the other end of the pier ballroom from time to time and he and his reputation were discussed endlessly among my friends.

He came from quite a wealthy background and his parents owned a large-ish family business. They lived in a posh part of town, in a big, detached house with a massive garden, and they all had posh accents. All the kids had been to public school and expectations of them were high.

What attracted me to him were his looks, obviously, but also his sense of otherness. He always looked a bit different from everyone else – he would wear stupid clothes occasionally, like a top hat – and he had a brilliant sense of humour and was very bright. And for someone like me, from a fairly rigid family, it was a bit like being in a cartoon, everything was so exaggerated.

A lot of local people thought he was a bit of an arse, and he probably was, but that didn't stop me, at the age of sixteen, being enormously attracted to him.

His sense of adventure was connected to the enormous amount he drank. I never saw someone so skinny put away so much beer. On a good night he could do fifteen pints no trouble, and this would lead to him shooting his mouth off at people and occasionally getting into trouble for it. However, I don't really remember him getting into any fights. I suspect people didn't think it was worth it, as you'd have snapped him in half with a small punch.

He was in a local band, who famously only ever did one gig, during which Dave fell off the stage and broke his leg. I didn't see it because I wasn't allowed out.

Helen and I were starting to explore the delights of Hastings nightlife. For a teenager, there was a huge amount on offer. There was an endless supply of eligible, hippy-looking men and nights of pure joy, dancing, flirting, drinking and snogging on the beach after last orders. Added to that, there was the Old Town, a warren of narrow streets containing three pubs which were heaving with people under the age of twenty, had a terrible reputation for drugs and therefore were enormously attractive. My favourite was the

Left: My mum would often leave my brother Bill and me in the park if we were being annoying

Right: Me aged six weeks. Rictus smile on Mother due to lack of sleep

Below: My granddad Ted and Maisie, my grandmother, practising their ventriloquist act...

Above: ...and my mum and dad having a go

Left: My dad obviously didn't like the photographer

Above: My mum would often leave my dad with us in the park too

Left: Our house in Clapham. Seems to be a burglar at the window

Left: Bill, a friend and me, about to go bonkers after some E-number licking. I'm the one with the curly hair

Below: Playing near the sewage pipe probably

Below: Cousin Neil, Matt, Grandma holding baby cousin Shelagh, Bill and me, looking remarkably cheerful for children who have been told to sit still

Right: I sometimes dropped off to sleep at school

Below: Obviously taken *before* sports day as I'm standing up

Above: We were often snapped with a horse's arse

Below: Trying to get the bastard to break into a gallop

Left: An early modelling contract for *Health and Efficiency* magazine

Below: My two brothers and me, school photo… they were kicking me under the table

Right: Yes, I was a nice
little girl once

Below: Benenden Primary,
on the village green. I'm
in pink, how humiliating,
fourth from the left,
front row

Right: Seem to have lost my bottom half

Below: Mum, Dad, Matt, Granddad Ernest, Bill and me on the cusp of hideous seventies fashion. Yes, that is a tank top

Anchor, a low-ceilinged, dark little pub with a brilliant jukebox and a crowd of Hastings hippies surreptitiously smoking huge joints in the corner. Hastings Pier also offered a series of (for us) romantic, famous bands about once or twice a month.

The most memorable nights I had seeing bands on Hastings Pier were:

T. Rex

Marc Bolan was every teenage girl's fantasy at the time and I couldn't quite believe I'd managed to get tickets, but we were very lucky because we got someone to queue for us as soon as they went on sale.

There were absolutely hundreds of lovelorn teenage girls there that night, and the atmosphere was charged with hormones. There was weeping, screaming, sighing, shouts of 'I love you, Marc!', pushing, shoving, waving, gasping, note-throwing, singing and every other element of a pubescent, psychotic love affair. When Marc Bolan came on stage, everyone exploded into a cascade of untrammelled emotion. He did all the hits we loved – 'Jeepster', 'Get It On', 'Ride a White Swan', 'Metal Guru'. I tried to get near the front, but was impeded by a scary, seething, histrionic, threatening mass of girls whose life depended on touching Marc.

Many girls fainted at the front and were dragged on to the stage, only to spring immediately to life and try to clutch on to Marc for all they were worth. It was weird to be in this tragic, sweating mass of unrequited love, because I've never gone down the road of un-attainable adoration. I prefer to at least have a decent crack at the object of my desire.

Golden Earring

Golden Earring were a Dutch band who had a massive hit in the seventies with a song called 'Radar Love', and for sheer energy and noise, you couldn't match them. At one point during the gig, the drummer leapt off his stool right over the drum kit and on to the front of the stage. It was amazing and to this day I still have no idea how he did it – he appeared to have taken off from a mini trampoline.

There were some quite scary greaser girls in the toilets at that gig, clad from head to toe in leather and wearing enough eyeliner to kill a whole laboratory of beagles. I made the mistake of going in on my own and got trapped when I came out of the toilet and could not make it to the door. There were about eight of them and one was predictably swinging a bike chain. And there was me in my patchouli-soaked Laura Ashley skirt and scruffy old Loon T-shirt, with no shoes on. I wondered if I was going to get out alive.

I decided there was no point going down the 'peace, man' route and that the element of surprise was best, so while they were looking me up and down and saying things like 'You fucking stupid little hippie,' I faced the biggest one and said in my bravest voice, 'Get out of my way or I'll kick the shit out of you.'

I think they were more amused than frightened at these words coming from the mouth of an apparent child of love, and it gave me just enough time to slip out of the door and hide in the crowd for the rest of the night.

The Kinks

The Kinks were just glorious. All I can really remember is their brilliant songs swirling round us, 'Waterloo Sunset' being my favourite. The crowd was very slightly more sedate and didn't indulge in hysteria like the T. Rex crowd. I went with Helen. We had spent ages getting ready in her bedroom and had put so much make-up on we probably looked like drag queens. After the gig finished, we thought we'd better find a cab. We had run out of fags and had just enough to buy ten No. 6 at the end of the pier. We put our money in the machine and the bloody thing jammed – so frustrating, as that was all the money we had left – and we were hopelessly banging the machine with our pathetic little fists when a charming voice behind us said, 'Can I help, ladies?'

It was Ray Davies himself, a knight in shining armour. He gave the machine an almighty thump and ten No. 6 came shooting down into the drawer. I have met Ray Davies subsequently on Jools Holland's radio show and, of course, related the story to him. Funnily enough, he didn't remember doing it.

The Crazy World of Arthur Brown

Arthur Brown had had a huge hit with 'Fire' in the sixties, and I suppose some would say he was past his best. But he put on a brilliant theatrical show, with the entire band dressed up as very strange things, ranging from a telephone box to a monk. Arthur Brown, of course, was famous for wearing a burning helmet on his head while he sang the song. This time, though, he was slightly more sensible and just leapt about looking scary. One doesn't normally associate seeing bands with having a really good laugh, but I did that night.

Gary Glitter

I actually saw Gary Glitter in my local park rather than on the pier, but he deserves a mention, particularly given recent developments. He tottered on stage in the highest pair of silver shoes I had ever seen and clad in a suit apparently made of BacoFoil. He looked bloody ridiculous. This was the age of glam rock, though, and pretty much everyone who came under its auspices looked extraordinarily silly. Glitter's big hits were 'Rock and Roll', 'I'm the Leader of the Gang' and 'I Love You Love'. He performed like a surprised Elvis with Parkinson's disease and his jerky movements and amazed expression made me laugh uproariously. I suppose it was much easier in those days for him to indulge his predilection for young girls as, let's face it, many pop stars did. I found the whole era of glam rock rather distasteful altogether and The Sweet always looked to me like they were only just on the right side of being hideously pervy. In fact, the whole experience of seeing Mr Glitter was more like staring at a noisy fairground ride than listening to music.

I have to be fair to my parents. They had made the effort to indulge me, up to their limit and much against their better judgement, and had allowed me to have a party at our house for my sixteenth birthday.

The party was like every teenage party has ever been – always slightly on the edge of out-of-control. My mum and dad went out for the evening and left us to it, with dire warnings of what would happen if there was any damage. They promised to come back late to give us a chance to really have fun. Then they broke their word and arrived back half an hour earlier than they had promised. As they opened the door, Mouse vomited out of it. They scattered people as fast as they could, leaving only Lucy's boyfriend passed out in his car and sleeping it off. But this wasn't good enough for my mum and dad who, I suppose, were worried about whether he would choke on his own vomit and insisted on phoning his dad to come and pick him up. The dad was not amused to be called out and gave the impression that he would far rather have allowed his son to sleep covered in sick. He had a somewhat grumpy exchange with my dad and hauled the offending teenager out of his car and took him home.

The fall-out from the party was what I remember as the start of serious battles between me and my parents. I spent a lot of time sulking and feeling hard done by, and as time went on things began to really escalate.

During the holidays, I got a job as a hop-picker. This was a job that was traditionally done by Londoners who would come down to Kent for their holidays, stay in appallingly cramped conditions and then somehow manage to look cheerful in those gorgeous black and white photos which picture an era long forgotten.

But things had changed by the time I started. Students and school children were the mainstay of the hop-picking industry. We were picked up at about six in the morning and driven out to Bodiam to the hop fields. I can't remember what time we finished but it was a very long day and I was bloody exhausted by the end of it. Again, it was hippy heaven. Lots of seventeen and eighteen year olds like me, who would get the tea going and make toast which was spread liberally with jam and then sprinkled with a few crumbs of dope to make the day go with a zing. Inevitably, there was lots of giggling. The days were long, glorious and hot and I loved it. Not many women did hop-picking, so there was a surfeit of boys. We worked in teams of three. One would drive the tractor, another would stand in a sort of crow's nest attached to the front of a trailer and cut the hops down and the third would hook the long strands of hops (or bines) between two metal rods at the front of the trailer. It wasn't that difficult, but it was quite monotonous and some days we got very bored. Very occasionally we would stand one of our hop knives upright in the ground and drive the tractor over it so we got a puncture. This took a good hour to mend, leaving us some time to lounge under the trees having a snooze.

I made some very good friends while hop-picking. My two main mates were Lucky and Baz, who didn't seem to do very much except get stoned. Lucky used to wear the most ridiculous hat in the shape of a teapot that some girlfriend had made for him. He and Baz spent a lot of the time seeing who could roll the biggest joint and laughing about things that probably weren't very funny to anyone else. What I loved about them was that they were so silly and neither of them would have harmed a fly. Lucky literally, because he was a Buddhist.

To a girl who had been brought up in an idyllic Kent village and not seen anything outside the boundaries of a fairly conservative human existence, they seemed very exotic. They'd travelled quite a lot and talked about India and South America. Compared with a lot of the boys I'd met in Hastings, who were ever so slightly loutish and whose horizons extended no further than the pub on a Saturday night, I felt very comfortable in their company. Not only that, there was no sexual tension between us at all. It was almost as if they were gay. Whether their libidos had been swamped by the amount of dope they smoked or they were just naturally semi-conscious in their approach to life, I don't know, but I enjoyed being with them so much it occurred to me to run away from home and take off with them as part of a trio. We talked about this at length and I fantasised about the three of us getting one of those painted caravans together and travelling round Ireland. They encouraged me too. In fact we very nearly got to the point of putting a plan together, and then it all went wrong at home . . .

After working together for a few weeks, my friends and I decided we'd all like to go out. Someone suggested *Last Tango In Paris* which was showing at the local cinema, the overblown, sexy, shocking Marlon Brando vehicle with some very rude scenes in it. I knew my parents would never agree to it, so I had to concoct an alibi (something I was very used to by now) to get me through, and so I told them that I was going round to see a friend from school to study. They looked slightly suspicious but accepted my story, and it was at this point that I made a cardinal error. I forgot to tell the friend in question, a very sweet girl called Jane, that she was my alibi for the night.

Off I went happily to the pictures with seven teenage boys of varying scruffiness. Alcohol and dope were hidden in rucksacks and we all sat in the darkness, feeling deliciously out of touch with reality as the ribald Parisian tale unfolded in front of us.

It seems to be my lot in life to be unlucky at moments of extreme deception, because after I had left, my friend Jane phoned my house to see what I was doing, having forgotten I said I was going to the cinema, and, on being questioned by my mum, let slip where I was and who with. This was in no way malicious. Coming from a liberal family, she had no idea that such a film would be off limits and was probably just being chatty.

I came out of the cinema, giggling and joking, to find both my mum and dad sitting in the car right in front of us, looking extraordinarily unhappy, to put it mildly. Knowing how scary my dad could be, I felt like legging it up the road and never coming back. But he grabbed me. There were some half-hearted attempts on behalf of my escorts to prevent me being hauled off into the dragon's den, but they were no match for my dad, who could comfortably have been described as incandescent at that point. His glowering anger was too much for any semi-stoned hippy. They melted away and left me to my fate.

This incident seems to have been the opportunity for my dad to demonstrate his rage about the way in which my life was going. When we got home, it absolutely poured out of him. He stood very still and shouted as loud as he could. And, bloody hell, was that loud! We covered my appearance, the way I smelled so appallingly of patchouli, my friends, my attitude, my school performance . . . the lot.

In his fury, he was obviously punting around for some way to confirm just what a huge disappointment I was to them and how changes were going to be made. I got a sense of my mum's ambivalence. I'm sure she was equally as angry and upset as my dad, but I think she might have handled the whole thing slightly differently. Especially considering what followed.

He told me to go upstairs and get all my clothes – the Laura Ashley skirts, jeans and scruffy T-shirts were a huge source of irritation. This I did and, to my amazement, he gathered them all up into a pile, walked out into the garden with them, got some petrol from the shed, poured it over them and set fire to the whole bloody lot. I could not believe it. Absolutely every item of clothing I loved sat in front of me consumed by flames and my identity sailed up to the heavens in plumes of thick, black smoke.

In among the clothes that were burning were some items I really loved – a white and grey long skirt which fitted perfectly and was admired by all my friends, a scruffy blue jumper, baggy beyond belief, which was almost like a comfort blanket, and a pair of green, very flared loons which had dragged on the ground so much they were straggly at the bottom and almost fringed.

I felt a mixture of rage, fear and disbelief as I watched all my stuff turning to ashes. I was too frightened to do anything other than stare stony-faced at the inferno, wearing my dressing gown because that was all I had left.

I slept well that night because emotional traumas don't keep me awake. If I am tired, which I was, I just go to sleep, whether the rabbit's just died or we are on the brink of a nuclear war. It's always been that way and it's great.

I can understand why my dad was so angry. After all, seeing one's only daughter emerge from a filthy film with a load of filthy hippies is enough to make the top of any dad's head blow off. As for the burning of the clothes, well, one way to see it is as an extreme version of Trinny and Susannah, I suppose.

The following morning a funereal atmosphere hung over the house. I, clothes-less, had to sit tight until my mum went off down to Marks and Spencer in the town and bought me some 'suitable' garments to wear. I don't really remember what these were, but they were generally of a bland and tweedy nature.

Things didn't really get much better. I was on the phone on the upstairs landing one evening, talking to a casual boyfriend, when my dad, again at the end of his tether, this time because Neil Young was playing rather too loudly out of my bedroom, came running up the stairs, told the phone receiver to fuck off, ran into my bedroom and drop-kicked my record player against the wall. I don't think that Neil Young album ever recovered, and neither did the boy on the end of the phone.

Once things had started to calm down a bit, I began to take liberties again. Dave and I had started to see each other a bit and one night he invited me to the pub for a friend's birthday. I told my parents some lie or other about where I was going. It all went swimmingly well until, on the way home, I realised I had lost my purse in the pub. There hadn't been much in it, so I didn't worry too much . . . until the next morning.

At around ten the doorbell rang. Everyone was around

and I answered the door. Standing on the doorstep was a big, unshaven Hell's Angel in black leather with various skulls and crossbones painted about his person. He was very tall, slightly chubby and had extraordinarily greasy hair. Apart from that, he was very attractive.

'Hello,' I said. 'Can I help you?'

In his hand he was holding my purse. 'Found this,' he said gruffly, 'thought you might need it.'

My first thought was 'Oh fuck, I've been rumbled,' and I grabbed it, said, 'Thanks very much,' and tried to shut the door in his face.

It was too late. My mum had arrived at the door.

'What is it, dear?'

Our anti-hero intervened. 'I was just returning this purse I found.'

A broad smile spread across my mum's face. 'Lovely,' she said and turned to me. 'Didn't even know you'd lost it.'

My heart was thumping and my brain was trying to will him not to tell her. 'Yes, I must have dropped it when I was out,' I said.

'Found it in the Anchor,' he said (the bastard).

The smile flitted away to be replaced by stoniness. 'Well, thank you very much,' said my mum. 'We appreciate it. Goodbye.'

I think Mr Nasty was hoping for a reward. But he was lucky he didn't get thumped, being the bearer of such ignominious news.

A three-month curfew ensued. There followed several weeks of sitting in my room, spilling bile into my diary and blowing fag smoke out of the window as my only entertainment.

If you are a teenager, staying in for three months is like being killed. It was unbearable. I was allowed to see a few friends during the day at weekends and I used to meet a friend, Kate, who lived just round the corner. I wasn't that close to or particularly friendly with her, but the ease of location was enough to bring us together. She was tall with long hair, John Lennon pebble glasses and white, almost translucent skin. One day we got talking about drug experiences. Someone had told me that you could make tea out of cigarettes for asthmatics and, because they had Benzedrine in them, they gave you quite a buzz. So I sent Kate off to Boots to buy them because she looked older, more studious and therefore more convincing than I did. I waited expectantly at home until she phoned me and said excitedly that she had got them.

I told my mum I was popping round to hers for a chat and arrived looking forward to trying something a bit spectacular. Kate's mum was also in, but, under the pretext of making tea, Kate filled a small teapot with boiling water and we took it up to her room. We weren't sure how many fags to put in the pot, so we plumped for three. They immediately disintegrated and as we didn't have a tea strainer, we were forced to pour out cups of tea with bits of tobacco floating in them. It didn't look very inviting. It didn't taste very inviting either – bitter and tobacco-y – but we forced it down and sat waiting for a result for about twenty minutes. Nothing happened, and I knew I had to be back for tea, so I left. I felt very slightly strange on the way home, but it was nothing particularly mind-altering, so I just forgot about it and the feeling passed.

After tea, the phone rang and I picked it up. It was a very angry Kate's mum, demanding to speak to my mother. I mumbled something about her being busy and slammed the phone down. Of course it rang again straight away and my mother, sensing that something was afoot, picked it up. She listened intently for about half a minute and then said something like 'Yes, I will indeed, yes, thank you.' She turned to me and I knew it was bad.

It seemed Kate had been far more affected than me by our 'tea' and, in a semi-hysterical state, had attempted to jump out of her bedroom window and had had to be pulled in by her mother. Obviously, to make herself the innocent in the crime, she had spilled the beans and blamed it all on me. It was my idea, I'd bought the cigarettes, and I'd made the tea and had virtually forced her to drink it. I protested my innocence, but it fell on deaf ears and, once more, I was grounded for a very long time.

Chapter 9

Out of my Mind

By the beginning of my second year at Hastings High School, battle had well and truly commenced. Arguments ranged from what I wore – as I had managed to sneak a few items of very unpalatable clothing back into my wardrobe – how little work I did, what my friends were like, where I wanted to go out to and what state my bedroom was in. I don't suppose it was particularly different from any teenager's bedroom. It wasn't dirty, it was just a mess, because I am a messy person. There were books piled everywhere, ranging from poetry to Dickens to detective novels, clothes all over the floor and records piled up or just lying around out of their sleeves. I think this is one area where we women differ hugely from men. I am very bad at putting things like CDs and DVDs back in their cases. Yes, I know it ruins them, but for some reason I don't give a shit – never have and never will.

At one point, my mum did that stereotypical thing that mums do: she read my diary. Of course, when are you ever going to find out anything you actually want to know when you do that? I suspect my mum was torn between wanting to allow me to be a private person and being desperate to know what I was up to. I don't blame her at all for doing it. It must have been an irresistible temptation and, as far as I know, she didn't actually go looking for it; she was 'tidying up' at the time. Still, 'tidying up' can be a euphemism for 'I was examining your belongings with a magnifying glass.'

I didn't really feel shocked, I felt embarrassed. Even I, as a teenager myself at the time, knew what a complete load of old cobblers teenagers write in their diaries, how badly written it is and how horrible it is to think of someone, even someone in the family, reading it.

There was a description of going to a party and taking LSD and the resulting mind chaos. Of course, I realise an icy hand must have gripped her heart when she read it, as the generations that separate us all necessarily dictate that our knowledge of the following generation's drug of choice is beyond our grasp. Thus my ingestion of 'acid' caused a combination of huge panic and anger.

From my point of view at the time, they knew nothing about drugs and were being completely histrionic. They drew a natural line through from smoking dope to heroin addiction via cocaine and speed. Inside, I knew drugs would never be my vice of choice, but it was impossible to convince them that I knew what I was talking about because their own young lives had been so relentlessly drug-free.

The experience itself had been amazing. I was at a party in a farmhouse with lots of people I knew, we were having a real laugh, someone had got some acid and so, with much giggling laced with pure fear, we all swallowed some.

I suppose I put any fears to one side in pursuit of a new and exciting experience. We'd all heard things about acid, people thinking they could fly and that kind of thing, but I think with the benefit of a bit of alcohol my confidence increased and I tried to feel positive and self-contained because someone had told me that if you are fearful in any way you will have a really bad trip.

It was a tiny little pink pill, very innocuous-looking. I didn't do any staring at it or any introspective internal arguing with myself, the room didn't start to spin as I considered the possibilities of what it could do, I just whacked it down my throat.

What a brilliant experience. Visually, everything became so much clearer and more colourful, as if lit from behind. Trees, particularly, took on huge significance for me and I stood staring at them for ages. Anything I examined closely seemed to take on a face. I remember staring at a plate of ham sandwiches which all had the face of the easy-listening American crooner Andy Williams and I began singing 'Can't Get Used To Losing You'. I also chatted with a Bob Dylan poster for some considerable time.

Yes, I know, bloody boring to watch. That's why people who take drugs are so dull. They just stand or sit staring blankly into the middle distance with a kind of goofy grin on their faces and they have nothing to say to you.

I realise that I was one of the lucky ones, and that I took a real chance by ingesting a mind-altering substance such as acid. The fact is that most people who take it survive emotionally intact, although some don't and become well acquainted with the inside of psychiatric wards. Because, in a basic way, it could be said that taking LSD is a bit like being psychotic. You certainly lose your grip on reality for a short period of time and your behaviour can be out of control. And there are some people who have some sort of congenital instability who take something like acid and it does seem to tip them over the edge into permanent mental illness. So this is not a manifesto for drugs. It was an amazing experience but I never willingly repeated it because, even then, I realised that something that was so powerful in terms of altering my mind had the potential to do enormous damage, and I didn't want to take the risk again.

However, this mind-altering experience drove another nail into the coffin of my good relations with my parents, and things began to speed towards the final countdown.

I feel sorry for my parents in hindsight. I don't think I was easy to deal with. For a start, I was so resentful, but, worse, I was self-righteous about it and that was quite a hard nut for them to crack. I was also stubborn and on a mission to make them feel bad and not give an inch. I suspect that because they were not of a generation in which teenagers rebelled by being sulky, hormonal and not very grateful for what they were given, they were really up against it. In their book, things were going from bad to worse. For my part, I felt in control and safe. Both of us were partly wrong.

The other thing I did as a teenager was a lot of hitchhiking, being short of cash and without a car. When I look back on this now, I am seized by fear, as the random nature of attacks on women in vulnerable situations like this means anything could have happened to me at any time. Perhaps the most memorable trip was from Hastings to Bexhill, a journey of about two miles, one Friday evening on my way to a party. A scruffy lorry stopped containing four men, all sitting on the front bench seat. They were Irish, ranging in age from early twenties to about mid-sixties.

'Where are you going, love?' one shouted out of the cab.

Seeing there were a few of them, an instinct made me say, 'Oh, it's all right, I'm nearly there, I can walk.'

They rejected this and two of them jumped out of the cab, making encouraging noises, and invited me to climb up and sit in the middle of them.

Note to Teenage Girls
a) Don't hitchhike; it's not worth the risk.
b) If you've ignored a) and you have any instinct

that something is wrong, don't get in out of
politeness, because you are probably right.

c) If you have ignored a) and b) and you get in, at
least give yourself an emergency exit, so if necessary you can dive out and leg it.

I, of course, had not followed any of these guidelines
and found myself in a four-Irishmen sandwich. Initially
they were playful and reasonably unthreatening, but
slowly the atmosphere changed and comments began
to be made about my looks, an arm went round me and
I began to wish I was a black-belt in karate.

I don't really know what made me say it, but I introduced into the conversation that I was at a convent and
when I left I was going to become a nun. I must be a
better actor than I think, because the atmosphere changed
again. The arm disappeared from round my shoulder and
an almost respectful mood emerged. They dropped me
off some two minutes later and I stood by the side of
the road feeling I had escaped something grim.

This enormous risk I had taken was so that I could
go to a party with Dave. Our relationship had moved
through various stages, from eyeing each other across
pubs, to tentatively chatting, to meeting in the pub,
to me being invited to stay at his house.

I'd managed to convince my parents that I was staying at Helen's house. Very occasionally this deception worked and I managed to get out for a whole glorious night. I met Dave at a nearby pub and we went on to the party, in some anonymous flat where several people were just lying around on cushions, a few were dancing and quite a lot were entwined, snogging. Lots of joints were being passed around and endless new ones were being rolled. I remember that being able to roll a joint was a bit of a badge of honour in those days, and it was frowned upon if you produced a loosely put together one that disintegrated in your hands or one that was so tightly rolled that nothing happened when you sucked it. Unfortunately, I was crap at it, having all the dexterity of someone wearing woolly gloves. Nothing was ever said, but disdainful eyebrows were definitely raised.

After the party, the story was concocted that if Helen's parents asked where I was the following morning, she would say I had stayed with someone else, and off I went back to Dave's house for our first night together. In the garden was a big shed, which was apparently called a summer house. It was very nice inside, with a bed, a table and chairs and cushions thrown about everywhere. I intended to leave early in the morning, as we had agreed that it wasn't the right time to 'meet the parents'. Having discovered they were up and about at seven thirty-ish, the alarm was set for seven and we drifted into an alcohol-fuelled coma. Of course, the alarm went off without either of us hearing it. I woke up and, when my brain had engaged and my eyes had focused, realised that it was more like eight o'clock. I was in a huge state of panic. My beau suggested that if all was quiet, the only place I needed to worry about being seen from was the dining-room window.

So I was up and dressed in seconds and ran as fast as I could across the lawn until I got near the house, at which point I dropped to my hands and knees and began to crawl, hugging the wall as if my life depended on it. Something made me look up at the dining-room window and I was greeted with the sight of the entire family standing, arms folded, at the window, gazing down at me as if I was some wounded slug crawling across their line of vision. I stood up and legged it.

I had kept Dave's existence a secret from my mum and dad because I knew what they would think. He wasn't that popular with my friends, I suppose because they could tell he was somewhat unreliable, to put it mildly. As friends always do, they were just looking out for my welfare – they didn't want me to be pissed about or hurt. And, of course, they were always there to act as a sounding board for endless analyses of:

1. Why he hasn't phoned when he said he would.
2. Whether he's shown any signs of lacking commitment.
3. What he said, what you said, what he said, etc., etc. Ad nauseam.

I didn't lose any friends because of Dave. They were quite happy to take a back seat and follow the course of the relationship as if it was a comic-strip romance come to life. And, of course, I'm sure they did endless gossiping about it, because that's what girls do. If a romance is up and running, friends have to be able to accommodate all the ups and downs of it. So one day they will concur with you, as you raise your eyes to the heavens and shout, 'He's a bastard, he's a bastard, I don't want anything to do with him,' and then the next day smile indulgently when you inform them it's all back on track and you're madly in love again.

I was in the grip of a grand obsession and had started to work out as many ways as I could to get out of the house and meet up with him. Most nights, I waited until my parents had gone to bed and, because the front door was locked and it was too risky to jangle keys, I went out through the kitchen door and out of the garage window. This was also the way back in. Unfortunately, one night, somewhat pissed, I was climbing back in and fell on the bonnet of my dad's car. Even though I wasn't big, it still made a pretty sizeable dent. I held my breath for the next day, but for some reason he didn't notice it for quite a while and then blamed it on something else.

Dave and I also spent a night in a so-called 'posh' hotel on the seafront. It wasn't really posh – I would imagine it couldn't compete with some very down-market hotels in London – but I thought it was posh because it stood on the seafront, had a sea view and was bloody massive. Added to this, I'd never stayed in a hotel without my parents before. And even then I use the term 'hotel' lightly. There would have been a couple of guest-houses on the Isle of Wight and one decent hotel in Jersey. By decent I mean no bed bugs and no prostitutes.

I was nervous when we checked in, feeling certain that we would be sent packing with the laughter of the reception staff ringing in our ears. But very soon you learn that hotels are not the moral arbiters of society – they are businesses like any other, and if you can afford to pay, they're happy to take you, whether you have a prison record as long as the pier or dodgy business to conduct.

We actually did pretend we were married and although we didn't go down the well-trodden 'Mr and Mrs Smith' road, we did call ourselves after a colour. I just can't remember whether it was Green, Brown or Black now. The girl on reception was roughly the same age as we were, and she looked rather envious at the sight of us hand-holding, scruffy hippies. I left all the arrangements to Dave. That posh, educated voice coming incongruously out of the mouth of a bedraggled ne'er-do-well always commanded a little more attention and respect. The room was secured and we had a lovely night there, sneaking out at about 7.30, hoping desperately we wouldn't bump into anyone we knew.

Eventually, I took the risk and told my parents I was seeing someone. Of course they wanted to know everything there was to know about him and so the fearful day came when I brought him back with me after a night out.

To say it didn't go well would be to say that the Second World War was a slight scuffle. My parents were waiting up for us and we were late. So when we arrived my dad did his 'what time do you call this?' routine. Although it is such a well-worn cliché, delivered by dads to their daughters since time began, it was still terrifying and infantilising, and I had rather hoped that my dad would put on a bit of a show for a visitor to the house, in the way you do when someone you don't know very well comes round. But there he stood, hands on hips, looking vaguely threatening to say the least.

I had primed them with a speech about how they probably wouldn't like him, would be put off by the way he looked, the way he spoke, how he dressed. All this would have been summed up by my dad as him being 'cocky'. And if there was one type of person my dad really wasn't keen on, it was a cocky bloke.

Dave's manner had always been la-di-dah at best, and his first sentence of apology had the words 'my dear chap' tacked on to the end. My dad, a true horny-handed son of the soil, quite reasonably took against being addressed as if he was a serf, and protested in a somewhat threatening manner. Unfortunately, my beau either thought it was a joke or he was too drunk to take it seriously and he used the phrase once more, where-upon my dad promised to hit him if he said it again. I'm sure you can guess the rest. He did say it again.

Time stood still for what seemed like an age. If I'm honest, I was pissed off with these two stags facing each other off. Why do men have to do this? It seems so tribal, so aggressive, and so utterly pointless. If I could have, I would have banged their heads together. The angry dad and the feckless lover competing in some sort of one-upmanship contest over me. I've always been a communicator and a smoother-over of things, I can't help myself, and the ideal scene which I had had in my head, where they sat down, had a drink together, talked about sport and had a laugh, was beginning to disintegrate before my eyes.

My dad was never one not to carry through on his promises. I saw a clenched fist come swooping towards Dave's jaw and he crumpled from the feet upwards, ending up sparko on the floor. All polite bets off, then.

When he came round a few seconds later, there was much talk from my dad of the 'never darken my doorstep again' variety. Dave rose to his feet with as much dignity as someone who's just been knocked over like a skittle can manage and left. My mum didn't get involved, but I could feel she was on my side. I felt like I'd been in a short Pinter play. I don't think we said much. I climbed wearily up to my room. Another jolly day in the Brand household over, and cue yet another enforced curfew for me.

The next time I spoke to Dave, I apologised over and over. But he was surprisingly chipper about it, and I presume being chinned by someone's dad is not a bad story to have in your arsenal.

I continued to fight my corner all the way, in a combination of titanic arguments, much sneaking out of the house, tears and me in my bedroom reading poetry and feeling like a tragic Brontë heroine, dying from love, but not TB. My knowledge of poetry was minimal, so I tended, magpie-like, to hop from school stuff to anthologies that my mum and dad had in the bookcase downstairs. Of course, for a while, the frustrated love ones were the best. A fair bit of Byron: 'So, We'll Go No More a Roving'. In my case, literally – roving was over for me for a bit.

Eventually, I think my parents were just so utterly sick of me refusing to cave in, don a tweedy two-piece and get a job in the library that they gave me an ultimatum: 'Ditch the loser or move out.' In some ways, these were the words I had been longing to hear. I still had quite some time left to go at school, but, after much discussion, it was agreed that I would get a job which gave me one day a week free and, weirdly, my school said they would allow me to come back once a week to study for my A-levels.

I think it must have been a very hard decision for my mum and dad to make, but there was all the background stuff going on with my dad's depressive illness to which I was not party. In truth, I was absolutely shocked that this was the decision they had been forced to make, having not realised I had pushed them so far. My discussion with them about it was minimal. They had made up their minds and I could take it or leave it. I think I was just seventeen at the time. I'm not sure why the school agreed to this bizarre arrangement, but my mother, as I have already mentioned, has very impressive powers of persuasion, and I presume she had them wriggling helplessly on the end of a hook before too long

A job was procured at the Department of the Environment and there then remained the question of where I would live. Dave found me a bed-sit near the seafront, a crumbling mansion with possibly the most interesting group of people ever to gather in one house.

Dave knew about the house because he used to live there himself and it was a fluke that a room was free. I think he was quite shocked that he had been responsible for this blowing apart of a family, and it terrified him. He impressed upon me that I wasn't his responsibility, which I understood, although I didn't have anyone else to rely on.

In the basement of this house there was the landlady, a sweet-looking, grey-haired lady who, rumour had it, dealt dope as a sideline. On the next floor was her daughter, a white single mum with a black baby, still frowned upon in Hastings in the seventies. Then there was me. Above me was a Rastafarian who played very loud reggae all day and night and above him, sharing one room, were five Korean cooks who played cards all night.

So I was all set to push out into the big, scary world when a minor disaster occurred. Dave got a job in west London, one he had applied for and accepted some weeks before I was ejected from the family home. It was a job as a residential social worker in a home for adolescents. It didn't require any qualifications, which was just as well, because he didn't really have any. Despite the enormous power of a wealthy family behind him, he had failed to make a mark in the education department. He rather liked working with naughty adolescents, possibly because that's what he was himself.

This meant that rather than us living together, he

would move, lock, stock and barrel, up to London and return to see me at the weekends. I had mixed feelings about living in the place on my own, but despite the tragedy of the breakdown of my relationship with my parents, I was really looking forward to moving out. I did feel sad, however, even though I needed a break from my mum and dad and they from me. I'm not sure what my brothers felt about it. Bill wasn't expressing much emotion at the time, although I know he was sad to see me leave Hastings. Also, I had taken most of the flak, and I expect he was worried he and Matt might mop up a bit more of it now I'd gone. Matt was more vocal and, although he didn't want me to go, he also agreed with the obvious: that we all needed a break.

So, one Saturday morning, my dad drove me down there, managed to bite his tongue about the suspect smells and grubbiness of the room and, after dropping my meagre belongings off, he bade me goodbye and I was left sitting on the bed, crying, feeling a mixture of fear, regret and excitement. I suspect that although on some level my dad was horrified about releasing me into the community, on another level he was mighty relieved that I would be out of the way. He did not throw open his arms as he bid me goodbye. It was all very self-contained and stiff-upper-lip-y. He preferred it that way. Me too.

After having been chained up for so long, it was surreal being on my own. Eating what I wanted, drinking what I wanted, smoking what I wanted.

I set to work to make the room my own and was given permission to paint it. Wanting to make a statement, I chose dark blue for the walls and red paint for the skirting (yes, I was mad). As usual, I didn't think about what I was doing and bought gloss for the walls. It was only after it didn't seem to be drying that I realised my mistake and as I didn't have any more money, I just had to leave it. It looked bloody hideous.

Despite the fact that I had the option of dissolving into a pissed, work-shy heap of patchouli-smelling, grubby Laura Ashley, I did manage to get myself to work on time and in a reasonable state. My job at the DoE involved paying DoE-employed cleaners and working out holiday benefits and sick pay. Well, I think that's what it involved; I wasn't really even sure at the time. It was one big skive. I'd get to work, have a coffee and a fag, do the crossword and cursorily glance at the top sheet of the pile of computer printouts. I love a cryptic crossword. My crossword of choice was the one in the *Telegraph* because it was the easiest, but I couldn't stand the paper itself, so I gradually weaned myself off it and tried to do the *Guardian* crossword, which was more cryptic and required a broader knowledge.

I remember once taking a call from a sweet woman who had been asked to pay back a million pounds. The poor woman was in a state of near hysteria, declaring there was no way she could afford it and crying snottily down the phone. What had happened was that the computer had generated too many noughts on a statement that had been sent to her about her sick pay, and she was being requested to pay back a million pounds of overpaid sick pay rather than a hundred pounds. When I reassured her that it was OK, that it was our mistake, she was so grateful and relieved that she started crying all over again. What surprised me was that it seemed obvious that a mistake had been made, and I couldn't believe her touching naiveté.

After a few months, I had settled into my bed-sit and job pretty well. Everyone at school was so envious of my freedom and there was a constant trickle of friends all attempting to escape their own particular brand of parental conflict at home and admiring the excessively shiny walls with barely disguised contempt.

Dave had never been the most reliable of partners.

He constantly turned up late or got involved in drinking sessions in the pub and arrived home several hours after he said he would. I didn't mind this too much, though. I never clock-watched and things were going along well. Glorious weekends in bed, drunken parties and hand-holding on the beach . . . paradise gained.

One night in the pub, unbeknownst to me, a local, very irritating and silly man slipped some LSD into my drink, a jolly pastime known as 'spiking'. I didn't realise this until I was walking along the road at about midnight, on my way home, and I happened to glance into a phone box in which stood a medieval monk swinging a cat backwards and forwards by its tail. It didn't occur to me that spiking might have occurred and I remember thinking that perhaps I had gone mad. Feeling rather scared, I decided to walk to my brother Bill's flat and stay there, as I didn't want to be on my own. At the time, Bill was training to be a quantity surveyor. I didn't understand what that was for ages (if you really want to know, he works out the amount of materials needed to construct a building). He had a small but perfectly adequate flat quite near my parents' house, although, like the abodes of most boys his age (he was nineteen at the time), it could have done with a bit more TLC cleaningwise.

As I got over the brow of the hill, about a quarter of a mile from his place, a bright-pink coach, its windows blazing with light, came up the road, mounted the pavement and came straight at me. I dived over a garden wall and found myself sitting in a flower bed facing a pack of huge, slavering wolves, all tied with leashes to a tree and straining to get at me. I picked myself up and ran the rest of the way, screaming and crying. Nobody came out to help.

My brother had read somewhere that vitamin C is a big help in counteracting the effects of something like LSD, so he poured orange juice down me all night and the effects gradually subsided. It was a terrifying experience and it only confirmed my worst fears about how dangerous acid could be. Perhaps, somewhere in the depths of my mind, some chemical thing had been triggered, and I couldn't stop myself from losing it and being very, very afraid.

The following weekend, the bloke who had spiked my drink came knocking at the front door of the house, shouting for Dave. I leaned out of the window and threw a bucket of water over him. Not a particularly effective revenge, but it made me feel better.

After about five months of my revolutionary new lifestyle, I arranged to meet Dave in a bar in the Old

Town on a Friday night. He always got the train back from London and went straight to a pub and I would go down there after I had got home from work and had time to change from Acceptable Drabness into my Teenage Witch About Town look. This consisted of dark clothes – a long skirt and long-sleeved T-shirt – messy hair, dark eye make-up and black lipstick, which I cherished, having spent an absolute bloody fortune on it in Biba in Kensington.

On this particular Friday, I had been allowed off work a bit early and headed down to meet him, thinking that for once I would beat him to the bar. The bar was in a basement and as it was early evening, it was dark and empty apart from one or two shadowy figures. I looked round thinking I must have arrived first. And then I saw Dave in a corner, wrapped round a really pretty girl with red hair, kissing her fiercely. I discovered what the phrase 'red mist' meant at that point.

Chapter 10

Bed-sit Betrayal

I did not just turn on my heel and walk out, because in the second or so that it took me to register the scene, a list of everything I had lost because of this man–boy flashed through my head. It was short but enormously consequential:

1. My home.
2. My relationship with my family.
3. My security.
4. My academic future.
5. My mind.

Yes, my mind had been slightly disturbed during those few months, and now I had lost it altogether.

Had I had a knife to hand, I suspect it would have been difficult not to use it. Thankfully I didn't, and I scanned the room for a weapon. The nearest thing to hand was a full soda siphon which was standing on the bar screaming to be used. I approached the guilty couple and before they had a chance to move or even react, I squirted them both full in the face with its contents. I have absolutely no idea what the resulting immediate fall-out was from my squirtiness because I exited stage left and made for home as fast as I could. When I got there, I got drunk and sat up all night playing cards with the Korean chefs and crying. They didn't seem to mind and were quite happy for me to get on with alternately sobbing and putting cards on the table.

Once this betrayal had occurred, much as I wanted to be forgiving, I just could not manage it, and I would constantly find myself ruminating on a way to physically or emotionally damage my erring partner. I eventually let him into my messy bed-sit with the very shiny walls and he prostrated himself and begged for forgiveness, insisting that the scenario which I had witnessed was purely a goodbye kiss and he was finished with the woman for ever.

In some ways, I suppose it was justice because a

previous girlfriend of his had been less than happy about my appearance in his life and had made her feelings plain on a number of quite scary occasions.

We rumbled on for a bit, but it dawned on me that the scene with the woman in the smoky bar had probably not been a one-off. But I was seventeen years old and I knew that my attempts to resist his charm, for charming he was, were just not going to work if I was always on tap, as it were.

You have to bear in mind that I thought he was charming because I was mad about him. I mean, some women manage to fall in love with murderers, so it is not the personality, necessarily, of the individual – it's your attitude towards him. To me, at the time, Dave was the perfect man: elfin, funny, bright, sparky, unpredictable, entertaining and enormously attractive. When it came to what he had done, he had just the right mix of regret and a take-it-or-leave-it attitude. And, of course, I fell for it, in a hook, line and sinker kind of way.

So I made a radical decision. I had plenty of time to think about it, as my life was fairly empty. My exams were finished (let's just say the marks 'D' and 'E' were good friends of mine) and my job in the civil service had crumbled to nothing following an incident at lunchtime, when I had gone to the very inexpensive club bar, had quite a few beers and been discovered asleep and dribbling on my desk in the middle of the afternoon. I was hauled up in front of the boss who spelled out the message that if I did not leave, I would be sacked.

I left.

So, while my duplicitous love was in London for the week, I hired a van, packed all my stuff into it and moved out of the bed-sit, leaving the few things that belonged to him and no forwarding address.

I returned to the place where I had always been so comfortable – Tunbridge Wells. I still had some very good friends from school. I knew I would be able to find a temporary place to live and a job and continue my life safely away from the source of my emotional torture.

After a relatively short time, I managed to get a job in a pub on the famous Pantiles, a historical pedestrian shopping street beloved by the Regency mob, which had a spring at one end where the dodgy-of-health would fill up bottles with water and hope that necking the stuff would make them better. My best friend Andy worked in the pub with me, and the couple who ran it, even though they were only in their mid-thirties, became like my second mum and dad.

I had known Andy since I was at school and had been introduced to him by a girl in my class, Jill. He was gay, enormously generous, funny, kind and is in my list of top five nice blokes of all time. His mum and dad used to run a grocer's shop in a village outside Tunbridge Wells, and I spent many a happy time at their place, one of the huge joys being that we were able to nip into the shop whenever we fancied and pick any bar of chocolate we wanted. Good job I wasn't brought up in a shop, I'd weigh fifty stone by now.

Andy knocked around with another gay guy called Paul, who also became a good friend. He could not have been more different – mercurial, thin, pretty and occasionally spiky. They were 'just good friends' but were a perfect foil for each other. Andy was big too and, at the time, had masses of frizzy blond hair. He always smelled gorgeous, as most gay men do, and wore fantastic seventies white suits and crocodile-skin pointy shoes. Most of my memories involving him are peppered with great, big, uncontrollable laughing sessions. The joy of having gay friends is that all those questions in your head about heterosexual men – like, is there something going on here? – are all brushed aside and you can indulge in a glorious, uncomplicated friendship with the male of the species.

He used to rescue me on occasion too. One night we were going to a party (thrown by the girl who had managed to insert a tampon during geography O-level, incidentally), and I had nothing interesting to wear. I had a lovely piece of Moroccan, green, fringed silk which, with the help of a few huge safety pins, was turned into a dress, pinned up on one shoulder. As everyone got drunker, I noticed our hostess looking at me with an evil look in her eye. She was quite pissed and obviously just could not resist her mischievous plan. She came over to me and, with one deft hand movement, pulled off my makeshift dress, leaving me standing in the middle of the party with just my pants on. Now, although I wasn't really overweight, neither did I have the confidence of a supermodel. I was absolutely mortified. Andy, quicker than a fat bloke should be allowed to be, was at my side almost immediately and enveloped me in a bear hug, while simultaneously covering up all the rude bits and edging me backwards towards a big curtain in which he wrapped me until I could be made decent again.

My tormentor, realising she had gone a bit far, came over to apologise, but I was so angry that before she could manage to get any words out, I punched her right in the gob. She keeled over backwards and was stunned, lying on the floor for a few seconds. I haven't had to use my right hook very often, but it was very effective on that occasion.

The married couple who ran the pub were called Dick and Monica. Dick was tall and thin with a sort of military moustache that made him look older than he was, for he had a charming, boyish face and a lovely smile. He was humorous, friendly and had endless patience with the punters. Monica was tall and slim with blond hair and an angular, pretty face. She perfectly complemented Dick. She was warm, very funny and a huge nurturer which was just what I needed, as I'd escaped from Hastings feeling bereft and had very little contact with my mum and dad. She used to bring us all a cup of tea in the morning before the pub opened and we would sit on bar stools, chatting, eating biscuits and slagging off the regulars. It was glorious. Their upstairs flat had a homey warmth about it that made me feel very secure and I was always up there watching telly and talking bollocks. The two of them made such a difference to my life and are a part of the happiest memories I have of this time.

Andy and I managed to find a flat on the Pantiles, and therefore it was about twelve steps from home to work – my perfect job. We settled into a life of very little responsibility, sharing the flat with a friend of mine from school and her boyfriend and spending long days in the pub – from ten till two thirty and then six till ten thirty, or eleven at weekends. I loved that job to pieces, apart from the morning shift, when a little crew of middle-aged men would take up residence at the bar at about eleven and talk bollocks for a couple of hours before the lunchtime trade drifted in. And, God bless 'em, were they dull. Some days I would take to inventing jobs just to get away from them, as they droned on about gardening, fishing, their sheds, their wives, their medical conditions, etc., etc. A few would appear in the early evenings as well and one night, as a little group sat at the bar, an irate wife appeared with a tray containing a cooked dinner, a pudding and a glass of water. She marched up to the bar, where her absent husband was positioned, banged the tray on to the bar and uttered the words, 'If you're not coming home, you can have your fucking dinner here.'

God, the poor guy, I thought, how embarrassing. Not a bit of it. He looked really pleased that someone had brought him his dinner and got stuck into it with relish – not quite the humiliating effect his wife had hoped for.

By this time, having put on quite a bit of weight due to the pill, I decided to take drastic steps to reduce it, so I embarked on one of those utterly ridiculous diets that as a seventeen year old are pretty easy to manage: three boiled eggs a day for a month. It had the desired effect and I knocked off three stone in that time, although I was grumpy as anything and a bit of a wind-creating machine. Having lost the weight and feeling really rather pleased with myself, I found one or two men who had previously ignored me giving me the eye. Unfortunately, these men were neither attractive to me nor in the least bit interesting. In fact, one of them was downright pervy and I suppose I subconsciously absorbed the message that being the focus of the male race's attention was not to my taste. The weight went back on pretty swiftly.

The flat we lived in was a beautiful Georgian place that sat above a posh shop selling very expensive fabric and the like. It had always felt strangely atmospheric and this led us one drunken night to hold a séance, with the aid of some letters hastily scribbled on torn-up pieces of paper and an upturned glass. We waited, as we had decided not to ask questions and just see if anyone turned up. Eventually, after some time, the glass spelled out the words 'Knowledge is not free'. Oh fuck, an old headmaster of Eton, I thought.

Curious, we asked the question 'What price is knowledge?'

At this point the glass spelled out 'Your life' and dramatically shot off the edge of the table. As we were all suffering from heightened excitement already, this incident made us feel quite shaken and we decided to go to bed. I got into bed feeling a bit of a scaredy-cat, turned the light off and tried to sleep. I had no success and the more I tried, the worse it became. I also had an increasing awareness that someone was in the room. As my head was hidden under the covers, I decided, very bravely I thought, to have a look round. As I peered out from the top of my eiderdown, I spotted a person in the corner of the room. A tall woman, dressed from head to foot in a greyish colour, with some sort of hat on. My heart wobbled and I reached for the bedside light. As light flooded the room, the person faded from view. I stumbled down the stairs to find my flatmate, Betty, also awake, and she told me that coat hangers had flown out of her wardrobe.

Now, I am quite prepared to believe that I was so drunk that I imagined the whole thing but it seems strange that something happened in two parts of the house at once. We moved not long after that.

I had been in Tunbridge Wells for about nine months and, apart from contact with a few people in Hastings, I had all but forgotten my old life, although I had found it a struggle not to ring Dave, whom I thought of often. But I knew it would go nowhere until he somehow sorted himself out and stopped leading the life of a relatively wealthy playboy.

And then one day, completely without warning, he walked into the pub while I was working. My poor teenage heart jumped in my chest and I became a human jelly. As soon as I got off work, we left together and went off to the flat to try to sort things out. He said he had been looking for me since I had left, but would not reveal how he had found me. I suspected he hadn't tramped round England like some wild-eyed Thomas Hardy character, suffering silently and sleeping out in all weathers, but that one of my friends had eventually caved in and grassed me up, but I never found out. I was so pleased to see him, although my friends weren't because, of course, my stories of his profligacy and unfaithfulness had led them to give him the label 'twat'. Had I been in my right mind, I probably would have agreed with them, but of course I wasn't.

I was somewhere in that psychotic nether region of the spirit known as 'being in love', and I didn't see sense and I didn't listen to anyone's advice. I'd written poems, for God's sake, and that's always a bad sign. So, despite a wealth of eminently sensible advice, I decided to reinstate cordial relations and go back to him. I made up my mind not to physically go back, though. Hastings is an interesting place which draws its sons and daughters inexorably back to a life they probably don't want and subconsciously, I think, like a young Oliver Twist, I was trying to get to London. (Sorry you've had to put up with two literary references in one paragraph. I assure you it's an aberration.)

So I saw Dave when I could and we wrote to each other. I felt torn between the two worlds, but I knew that if he drew me back in, it would end badly, which I'm sure my parents were anxious about too.

And now a grown-up job was required, as working full time in a pub was not really the career path I wanted to head down. With my friend Julia, I got a job working for Dr Barnardo's, at a complex of small houses, all of which were children's homes.

Julia and I had been in the same class at school. She was, and still is, such a funny person: cynical, quick, very bright and really good fun to be with. She was the perfect person to work with, as she kept me and the kids entertained and was always coming up with great ideas to stave off the boredom. One day she suggested we have a blindfolded food-tasting competition, whereupon we made up the most revolting combinations of food you can imagine, like salad cream, cornflakes, jam and sausages, and the kids had to put a blindfold on and guess what was in each bowl. They loved it and, amazingly, none of them was sick.

Each house had a married couple who lived there permanently plus two extra staff members, normally women, who were known as 'housemothers'. Bloody hell, I was only eighteen or nineteen at this point and certainly not ready to look after a load of kids.

I had no conscious reason for wanting to work with deprived and orphaned kids. I had worked in that field before because my mum was a social worker, and I found the pace and emotional involvement required for that sort of work very satisfying.

We had about eleven kids in the house. Poor little buggers, the lot of them, with various emotional problems. There was no washing machine for a while, so all the washing had to be done by hand, and with one child regularly jumping from bed to bed and pissing on the other kids while they were asleep, there was quite a lot of it. The couple I worked for were nice enough but would sometimes go away for the weekend with their own kids and leave me or Julia in charge. As we were teenagers, they suspected the worst and obviously thought we would spend the weekend chatting on the phone, so they locked the office with the phone in it, cutting off our only method of communication. This meant that in order to contact the outside world, one had to catch a passer-by or go to one of the other houses with *all* the kids in tow. Shopping was the same. I had to get on the bus with about eleven kids, including a toddler and a baby, and try to shop while stopping them gobbing, throwing things or fighting.

Just getting the little buggers out of the house was an achievement in itself. There were three sets of siblings: a brother and sister (sweet and lovely looking, they got adopted fairly quickly), two brothers with learning disabilities who were quite a management problem (they didn't get adopted) and another set of brothers who were just plain naughty (they didn't either). (Incidentally, I met the older of the last set of brothers in Camberwell about twenty years ago and he told me he was working as a pimp. I was so proud.) Then there was a baby in a pushchair and a toddler who needed to be strapped into a buggy of some sort too, or he would have dived headlong into the road, because that's what toddlers do. I seem to remember I had some sort of makeshift strap which I tied to his arm to stop him legging it off into the crowd.

It took a bloody age to get them all to the bus stop, with one child pushing the toddler's buggy and me with the baby. Then both pushchairs had to be folded up when the bus came and the whole lot herded on board. Trying to marshal them all round the supermarket and stop the shoplifting and the eating of scraps was a task beyond human endurance, hence I think I only ever took them all out like this twice and if we didn't have enough food in I just improvised with whatever was in the cupboard rather than face it again. I virtually needed counselling after these trips.

I was really lonely there sometimes. Once I asked the milkman in for a cup of tea, I was so desperate for human contact. Rather wisely perhaps, he declined.

One weekend, one of the kids, a strapping fifteen year old with slight learning disability, came downstairs at about eleven thirty while I was watching telly and announced, 'I've hurt my penis, can you have a look at it for me?'

Well, obviously, on my own with a boy nearly as big

as me, a penis examination didn't really grab me. I managed to break into the room with the phone and called Julia and asked for back up. She arrived twenty minutes later and we did the examination together. Nothing wrong at all and I'm afraid, more due to anxiety I think than anything else, we were hysterical for about an hour afterwards.

Dave, due to work commitments in London, didn't really manage to see me very often. He was still working in the same residential home and had a rather gruelling shift pattern. You may think we had cosy chats about our very similar jobs, but we didn't really. I don't think either of us wanted to talk about it outside work. I supplemented his meagre presence with a couple of on-off relationships, one with a delightful ceiling suspender who was no-nonsense, good fun and a joy to be with.

Do you want to know what a ceiling suspender is? Well OK then, they put ceilings in that are lower than the existing ceiling, I presume to save money on heating. This is normally done in old houses with very high ceilings, like your Georgians and Victorians.

My time with the ceiling suspender didn't particularly involve any exciting social events. We went to the pictures and pubs and had dinner quite a lot with friends. It was normal and lovely.

By this time, I'd found myself a perfectly adequate bed-sit in a leafy road full of huge Victorian houses. It was on the ground floor and my bed was next to the big bay window. On summer nights I often forgot to draw the heavy curtains. One night I was rather foolishly watching Hitchcock's *Psycho* on my own at one in the morning. I'm slightly pathetic on the horror film front. I've always wondered why it's considered so entertaining to see (mainly) women butchered in a variety of ways. Still, Hitchcock was always at the epicentre of the genre and there was nothing else on. So I steeled myself for the shower scene, although I could feel my heart beating faster. Just as the killer struck and my fear increased, there was a loud banging on the window and I looked over to see a leering face. I screamed my head off until I realised it was the ceiling suspender, who had crept up to the window and watched the film through it, the bastard, until it got to the shower scene.

Suffice it to say, we had words.

I chugged along at Barnardo's for a while, occasionally seeing Dave, although it wasn't going well. I suppose after everything we had been through, the curse of familiarity was setting in. We'd known each other for three years by now, so the initial flush of excitement had worn off ages ago.

I enjoyed the job, even though it was hard work and the hours were long. It was important to party hard too, I told myself, because I was only nineteen. And party we did. There was a group of about ten of us who would meet at the weekends and find something to do. We would drive out to country pubs, go back to someone's flat and put loud music on and dance, or go to Tunbridge Wells's premier nightclub, the Tropicana. At this time, my gay friend Andy was working in a wine bar, so often we would stay late there, just talking rubbish and having a laugh.

One woman in our group, Sarah, was a bit older than the rest of us and could have worked as a model, she was so beautiful. Her drinking caused her to behave in a rather mad and uncontrolled way, however. One weekend in the summer, she and I decided to do a bit of raspberry-picking. We soon got bored with it and repaired to the pub. In the pub we met two posh blokes, one of whom had recently taken over a National Trust stately home, and they invited us back for a drink. They cracked open several bottles of champagne and Sarah and I got completely slaughtered. Sarah was supposed to be working in the wine bar that night, so at about six o'clock we staggered out and fell into her butterscotch-coloured MG.

Of course, she shouldn't have been driving. Neither of us were wearing seatbelts and we went haring round the narrow country lanes in a highly dangerous fashion. After we'd gone a couple of miles, a car overtook us and flagged us down. We stopped and a rather officious middle-aged man got out and walked over. He told Sarah he had been following us and she was obviously drunk and should pull over until she sobered up. We tried to look serious but we were giggling like five year olds. As soon as he disappeared round the corner, we roared off again and as we came up to some red lights at Pembury, Sarah wasn't paying attention and shunted right into the car of the man who had told us off.

Sarah, fearful of being caught, as she was already banned from driving, got out of the car and legged it down the road. I had hit the dashboard and was bleeding copiously from the face, but I was still giggling hysterically. About a hundred yards down the road, Sarah's escape was curtailed by two policemen who had clocked her car at the lights, knowing it well, and they arrested her. I was driven as far as the police station with her and then shoved out to make my own way home. Some years later, Sarah died in mysterious circumstances in a South American jail, her whole life seemingly a long and tragic but very exciting novel.

One night I had been to a fancy-dress party and arrived home very, very, very drunk. I somehow convinced myself that I didn't want to go straight to sleep, despite the fact that I was virtually unconscious, so, having run out of change for the electric meter, I lit a candle next to my bed and switched on the telly. But within seconds I fell into the deep sleep of inebriation.

I'm not sure whether it was smoke or heat that woke me, but I sat up with a start and realised that my bed seemed to be on fire. I had knocked a blanket on to the candle and it was smouldering. So, as one does in these situations (like they happen all the time), I staggered to my delightfully minuscule kitchenette/evil-smelling cupboard, filled a jug with water and poured it over the smoulder. Sorted.

I got back into bed and went to sleep again. I'm not sure how much later I woke up, but it still seemed really hot and there appeared to be a glow coming from under my mattress. At this point, I did an extremely stupid thing that I wouldn't have done if I'd listened in physics lessons or not been pissed out of my head: I lifted up the mattress to inspect it. As soon as the oxygen hit it, the whole bloody thing went out of control. The curtains caught fire, the telly exploded and suddenly I was Miss Havisham in my own version of *Great Expectations*.

Chapter 11

Bed-sit Blow-up

At the point the curtains burst into flames, immediate sobering-up occurred and I thought that I'd better do something. I knocked on my next-door neighbour's bed-sit door and he opened it in his pyjamas – a sweet, rather unassuming man. I tried to play things down somewhat and said something like 'I've got a small fire in my room.' Wearily, and somewhat pissed off about being woken up, he walked the few steps across the hall with me and opened the door to my grimy little bed-sit to be presented with a raging inferno which had really taken hold. For a mild-mannered guy, he managed some impressive swear words and ran to the phone box in the hall and dialled 999.

The situation continued to progress surreally and, as I hadn't fully sobered up, I watched the resulting chaos through the protective gauze of inebriation, which was a big help, as the full force of it didn't hit me until sometime during the following days.

The fire brigade and the police arrived within minutes. I don't think they really had much excitement in Tunbridge Wells, so when they got there it felt a bit like being assailed by a combination of the SAS and some overgrown schoolboys. Enthusiastic to a fault and armed with big, grown-up equipment, they set to work. I was taken off at this point, a slightly gooey, sobbing heap, wearing my nightie and a coat with the arm burned off. A very sweet policewoman shoved me in the back of a police car and put a packet containing ten fags and a lighter in my hand, and I sat in the car and chain-smoked the lot.

Meanwhile, the boy scouts with hoses had run rampant in the flat and by the end of their ministrations, what hadn't been burned was soaked in water and ruined. They had broken the big bay window and charged in, all hoses blazing, and the fire was out in a matter of minutes, I suppose.

I suspect my sobbing had reached a slightly worrying/unmanageable stage because I was then taken to the local hospital's casualty department and given some sort of pill to calm me down. Then they agreed to deliver me to a friend's house for the night. They tried to call in advance but no one answered, so we ended up on the doorstep at about three thirty in the morning, while a policeman holding what probably looked like a bedraggled bundle of damp, burned rags rang the doorbell. As soon as the door was answered by the boyfriend of my friend, it became apparent why they hadn't answered the phone – they were having a bit of a 'sesh', as we used to call it. So much highly pungent smoke of the illegal variety escaped out of the door while we stood there, I'm surprised the policeman didn't faint, but he stalwartly stood his ground, refusing to acknowledge that criminal activity was taking place, and I thank him for that. The boyfriend was handed the bundle of rags (me) and I was escorted knackered, weeping and pissed into the house, where his girlfriend and my friend Andy were. Andy was staying there temporarily, and I climbed into his sofabed with him and dropped off.

The next morning, it has to be said, my life looked pretty bleak. I had lost everything, including my guitar, which I would tunelessly strum occasionally, trying to sing Dylan and Neil Young songs, all my clothes and

Left: Fags and the papers, my two favourite hobbies

Right: Looking like a teenage shoplifter in a photo booth

Below: Bill, me, Matt, Maisie and Aunty Paddy...well into seventies fashion horror at Bill's wedding

Left: The Cheshire Respite care gang, looking relentlessly cheerful in front of a miserable van

Below: On a boat just about to vomit

Left: Yes, I did feel bloody ridiculous

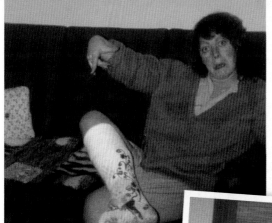

Left: Broken foot after pissed fall off fence trying to break into nurses' home

Below: Pointing at my breakfast

Below: With Ian

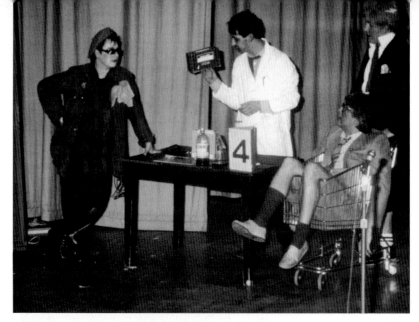

Above: As an unconventional Peter Pan in hospital panto

Below: As Mrs Drudge in *The Real Inspector Hound*. Leading lady: thin, blonde and pretty. That's radical

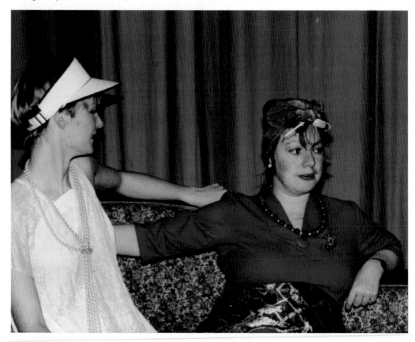

Left: My brother and his wife, the 'German contingent', and my mum. See, no towels on the drive

Below: Matt and me with Dad. I'm looking to see what's for tea

Below: At a wedding. Not mine

Left: Caught having a wee

Below: On another boat having just vomited

Left: In Rome playing lookey-likeys. Bit cross I'd shaved my beard off earlier

Left: When I was doing this outside the Louvre, a French bloke shouted out, '*C'est la même!*' Sarky bastard

Below: Morning after a fight in the student bar

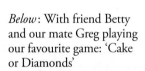

Below: With friend Betty and our mate Greg playing our favourite game: 'Cake or Diamonds'

Wearing contraceptive coils in my ears, for some strange reason

my big (to me) collection of about two hundred records. I hadn't really ever been a dedicated materialist but from that day onwards I've never allowed myself to get too attached to things, because I suppose I have assumed that at some point they will disappear in a puff of smoke (literally).

What I'd grab in a fire these days:

1. Husband and children, obviously.
2. Cats.
3. Computer. One exploded recently and, as I am not a nerd, I hadn't backed anything up.
4. My little orange book of jokes. Unlike Bob Monkhouse's book, which was a big, leather-bound jobbie, mine is a series of small red memo books stuck together with Sellotape.
5. The telly. I love watching telly so much. I think this is probably because it was rigorously limited when I was a child, so I tend to see it as a forbidden delight and will watch any old crap on it, apart from the Budget, which is so dull that not even I, Telly Addict, can stomach it.

Back to the story. I didn't go to work the next day. A friend called in to say that I wasn't in a fit state and, besides, had nothing to wear, and she reported back to me that the house parents I worked for didn't seem too happy about the fact that I had taken a day off for a mere fire, in which all my belongings and my accommodation had been consumed.

My friends had a whip-round and I managed to get a few items of clothing together and set off for work the following day, only to be greeted with a slightly cold attitude and obvious dissatisfaction that I had not been there the day before. To say I was in a hyper-sensitive state doesn't really describe it adequately and, of course, a row developed, the end result of which was me advising the two of them that they could stuff their job 'up their arses' and walking out of the place in the most dignified way I could manage.

The complex was quite a way from the centre of town and, as I strode angrily along, it suddenly hit me that I had no home, no belongings and no job. The future didn't look bright or orange; it looked pretty black.

I didn't really regret leaving Barnardo's. I felt I had 'done my time' and, given the circumstances, the fire was probably timely in the sense that it gave me the boot up the arse that I needed to move on. I missed the kids and Julia, but not so much that I wanted to go back.

I suspect some people in this situation would have sat down at the side of the road and sobbed. For some reason, I didn't. I'm a fairly pragmatic person who tries to take life as it comes, and unless you are completely alone in the world – and that must be awful – I think you can always find someone who will help you out. I am Mrs Do-As-You-Would-Be-Done-By and I would hope that I have given enough support to friends and family for them to return the favour. So, as the song goes, it was in my nature to pick myself up, dust myself down and start all over again.

So I did what I think everyone would do in that situation if they could. It is the natural reaction in times of extreme distress. A little girl's voice in my head kept repeating 'I want my mum!'

I called my mum from a phone box halfway along the road. As ever, she took the news pretty calmly and matter-of-factly and told me to hang on in there and that she would pick me up. Sure enough, forty-five minutes later, she came bowling along in her red MG Midget, with the roof down, scooped me up and ferried me back home.

'Back home' at that point was an isolated cottage up a long drive in rural Sussex, near the curiously named village of Herstmonceux, which has a castle and a well-known observatory. Once there, I took on a series of unpalatable and dull jobs while I tried to get myself back on my feet.

I've never been a big fan of isolated country cottages and, despite the beauty of the surroundings, I couldn't really settle there. There were beautiful cornfields in front of the house and verdant woodland behind it, and yet an atmosphere of foreboding seemed to hang over the place. My parents were back together at that point, having separated a few times, and it looked like this recent reconciliation would probably only be temporary too.

The atmosphere between my parents was not easy to cope with. Even though they tried hard to hide it, it was difficult to ignore the situation and we knew things weren't right. I think a parental separation inevitably makes children insecure, and it doesn't matter what age you are. Although I couldn't have put my finger on the effect it was having, I felt slightly anxious a lot of the time and a bit worried about my dad. I think, on the whole, without wanting to diss dads, in a traditional household, the mum is the centre of it all and if that piece is taken out of the jigsaw, things tend to fall apart. There is an argument for and against separation. It's 'for the sake of the children' versus 'splitting to create a better atmosphere'. I would always hope that couples who can't live together would seriously consider separating, because, in the long run, the acute pain of that is easier to cope with as a child than the chronic, long-drawn-out pain caused by a bad marriage. What seem to be the most important elements are that you are as truthful as you can be with children without offloading all the crap on to them, you don't force them to take sides and use them as allies and you reassure them that it's not their fault.

My mum and dad played their cards very close to their chests, so we would only be told that my mum was leaving the day before it happened. My mum did not confide in me and I don't feel she should have done. I know many mothers have a sort of 'best friends' relationship with their daughters, but I've always felt this was a bit inappropriate and slightly cringey. It takes away any sense of authority from the parent, which they need in order to be the grown-up in the relationship.

One incident that occurred while I was at the cottage made me roar with laughter. Knowing my dad loved Peter Cook and Dudley Moore, my brother Bill bought him *Derek and Clive Live* for his birthday. This was a shocking album at the time because it was so utterly filthy and included tracks with such a degree of swearing and rudeness that the right-wing press had thrown their hands up in despair and alarm.

My dad didn't know any of this, so he suggested we put it on and listen to it together. We all sat round and on went the first track, which was a conversation between Pete and Dud about the worst jobs they'd ever had. When we got to 'pulling lobsters out of Jayne Mansfield's bum' off came the record, an embarrassed silence filled the air and it was never mentioned again.

Not one for filth, my dad, and I'm sure he hasn't found it easy to listen to the more extreme elements of my comedy but, all power to him, he never mentions it.

One day, as my dad was wandering round the woods at the back of the house, he discovered a complete set of women's clothing scattered over a small area, some draped on bushes and some on the ground. My dad had watched enough TV detective series to know you didn't disturb evidence, so he left the stuff there. A call to the police and an investigation elicited no further information. Well, that finished me off psychologically and I couldn't wait to leave the place.

I worked for a little while at a local plant nursery, a very demanding job which involved pulling the heads off chrysanthemums, I suppose to encourage the main bloom to grow by discarding the smaller, less attractive ones, although my knowledge of gardening is minuscule. That job lasted the blink of an eye. I also worked briefly in a local French restaurant, with a predictably temperamental chef. I was the kitchen helper, his wife waitressed and he cooked – far too few staff for the size of the restaurant.

One day he was ordering me around the kitchen in his usual fascistic style. Normally I just got on with it, albeit silently and grumpily. However, that day, whether it was due to hormones or just plain tiredness, I was on edge. He knocked a big bowl of garlic that I had just peeled onto the floor by accident and turned to me with the words 'Pick it up.'

I wouldn't have minded picking it up had there been an apology, a please or both, but I was in no mood to be treated like some Gollum-type slave. So I kept quiet and patiently picked it all up while he stood there and watched, rinsed it in the sink, dried it, put it back into the bowl and then emptied the bowl on the floor and left the kitchen and the job with the words 'You pick it up.'

I will work as hard as I can, twenty-four hours a day if I have to, but I cannot abide anyone treating another human being like a piece of dirt, whatever the context. I realise I had the privilege of being able to walk out of that job without incurring any lasting consequences. I'm aware there are many millions of people who can't, and I feel desperately sorry for them.

Anyway realising that I missed the town, I decided to return to Hastings, where my brother Matt was living. Matt would have been about seventeen or eighteen at the time. He was a sensitive soul, very into his music and not desperately into school. At the time he had a job as a court clerk and was not that keen on the job either, because it was dull. He just saw it as a means to an end, so he could earn money to entertain himself at the weekend.

One night he was at a party and someone told him a couple of guys wanted to chat to him outside. He was a bit of a hippie at the time – long hair, flared jeans, colourful scarf – and very good looking. He went outside and the door slammed behind him. There were two squaddies in front of him who just didn't like the look of him. They, not to put too fine a point on it, proceeded to kick the shit out of him. He was in a very bad way and despite screaming for help, the music from the party was too loud to bring anyone out until the damage was done. His face was a mess and he was bruised everywhere. I suspect that this incident was responsible for what happened next in his life. He upped and left England and went to work on a kibbutz, and he has never lived here since. In Israel he met a Dutch girl and ended up in Holland for a bit and then met a German girl, Bibi, whom he subsequently married. They have a son, Max, who's now grown up. My German family has given me intense pleasure. Bibi's dad, Helmut, was a warm and lovely guy, an ex-soldier who was shot during the Second World War while in Czechoslovakia and marched to Russia, where he remained until five years after the war. He used to tell such colourful tales of his time in Russia and we all loved him. Sadly he died a few years ago.

Matt and I get on very well. He is good fun and takes life at his own pace.

When I went back to Hastings, I had nowhere to live initially so I moved in with Matt who was existing in one room. He did, however, have a big sliding wardrobe, so we put some bedding in there and at night I would ease myself in and close the sliding door. It wasn't comfortable in the slightest but it did for a few weeks.

Eventually Matt and I shared a flat together and had

a lovely time. Dave, my beau, had also moved back to Hastings by then, but I was dubious about rekindling a living-together situation. So I occasionally stayed with him, but as this was during the winter and his room seemed colder than an industrial fridge, I wasn't there often.

After a few weeks in the new flat, I didn't feel too well. I had a persistent pain in my abdomen which my GP rather conveniently ignored, advising the usual two paracetamol. One night the pain became so unbearable that my brother called an ambulance. I was taken off to casualty and it turned out to be peritonitis, for which I had to have an emergency operation. Looking back, what I remember most is that the non-smoking patients had a lounge with a colour telly and us lepers only had a black and white. I moaned non-stop at the time, but even a decent hospital room and not some rubbish-strewn fire escape eight miles away would be good these days.

I got a job as a nursing assistant in a huge residential institution for adults with learning disabilities. It was a Victorian building housing Victorian attitudes and the twentieth century seemed a faraway dream to most of the poor bastards who actually had to live there. Most of the staff were nice, but they had been driven into submission by a couple of scary senior staff. Neglect and disrespect were our constant companions and occasionally we strayed into sitcom territory, as the elderly gardener was rather partial to displaying his genitalia to any female under the age of seventy. The first time this happened I was rather shocked, but it became such a regular occurrence that I thought it was quite entertaining, although I wouldn't have wished it on anyone younger.

All the male residents had their pockets sewn up so as to avoid any embarrassing pocket billiards incidents and their hair was all the same style, taking as it did inspiration from Vidal Sassoon's pudding-bowl period. The women weren't really allowed to be women, although they would occasionally get their own back. One pure delight of a grumpy resident took to hoarding used sanitary towels in a carrier bag and chucking them at people she didn't like. She was once taken aside by a store detective in Woolies because she'd made a grab for the Pick 'n' Mix. I saw her hand go into her trusty carrier, almost in slow motion, and I began to run towards them, my warning shout seemingly becoming distorted and slowed down. I was too late – she'd already taken one out and aimed it at the detective's head – and I had to work enormously hard to convince the manager of the store that it would be all right for us to shop there again. I only pissed myself laughing once we'd got outside Woolies.

I saw things that, although they weren't deliberately cruel, really upset me. One poor woman had a plaster so tightly wound round one of her toes, which was left on for weeks, that by the time anyone realised something was wrong (by the smell), her toe was hanging on by a thread.

Perhaps my most dramatic contribution to the lives of the residents was the day I took them swimming at a local public pool. They were all having a lovely time splashing about, and one of the other staff said to me that she thought they would really appreciate someone showing them what diving was all about. I had always loved swimming and diving and had done a lot of it at school, so diving off the edge of the pool seemed like a piece of piss. I came out of the changing room in my cozzie, got their attention, stood halfway up the pool and announced that I was going to show them how to dive. I didn't go far enough up the pool, though, and as I executed a perfect dive, I realised it was too shallow. I hit the bottom, my top teeth went right through my face and I came up out of the water almost knocked out and in terrible pain. However, the main emotion I felt was embarrassment at being such a tit. I did my best to laugh it off as they clapped and cheered, but then noticed there was a small ring of crimson round me which was expanding by the second. Seeing my own blood made me feel faint and I was eventually dragged out of the pool, the sound of cheering and the sight of admiring faces the last image I remember.

In casualty, I was informed that my face was too swollen for them to use a local anaesthetic, so I had to endure a few minutes of agony as someone laboriously sewed up the hole under my nose. Not only that, a charming and huge scab formed between my nose and mouth and the effect of that plus the swelling gave my profile a gorilla-ish character. This lasted about a month and despite imaginative ideas to hide it – like wearing a scarf, Lone Ranger-style, over my face (too much laughing) or simply holding my hand up to cover it all the time (simply not practical) – I just had to put up with looking like an extra from *Planet of the Apes*.

Eventually I felt the line had been crossed at work when I saw one of the staff standing outside the women's bedroom watching them all getting undressed for bed. I made a complaint about this and was told obliquely that they weren't interested in what I had to say and as I was a recent addition to the staff, I might as well leave.

I did and pootled off back home to my mum again.

Chapter 12

Rosebed Rally Driving

Thankfully, I didn't have to move back into the house of fear tucked away down the lane. My mum had moved on her own to a lovely gothic cottage in a village about ten miles away, and she managed to get me a job at a residential unit for adults with learning disabilities. The place could not have been more different from the Victorian horror I had worked in previously. It was modern, light and airy and the staff seemed to be in touch with the twentieth century, which was a huge relief. The residents seemed happy and settled and there were no shenanigans going on. It's an indication, I think, of how much difference the management of these types of places makes in setting the tone of the care that is given.

At that point, I was trying to learn to drive and some days I persuaded my brother Bill, who was only down the road in Hastings, to come and pick me up from work so I could drive home.

I had had five driving lessons in Hastings already, with a cheery middle-aged guy who seemed totally un-flappable, which I suppose is a very useful character trait to have in that job. Most days he would greet me, plonk a pipe in his mouth and off we would go, chugging painfully slowly round the streets of Hastings, with him gently barking instructions at me. However, one day when I turned up for my lesson, I was told he would be about ten minutes late. Eventually he appeared from the little room and we got into the car. He looked slightly flustered and his hair, normally combed to within an inch of its life, was somewhat awry.

I asked him if he was all right and he explained that the previous pupil, on his second or third lesson, had come up to a T-junction in a busy area and rather than turn left, as he had asked, had somehow got his foot stuck on the accelerator and shot forward across the road and right through a shop window.

The car had been totalled but the instructor and learner were, thankfully, unharmed, although quite shaken up. And our brave hero had taken a mere ten minutes off with a cup of tea to steady his nerves and got straight back in the saddle, as it were, to give me a lesson. I tried really hard not to drive into a lamp post that day.

One day Bill arrived to pick me up from work in his car. It was a beautiful sunny day and all the residents were out in the garden. To be honest, I had bigged up my driving skills far too much. I thought I was the Charlie Big Potatoes of the road and an excited little gang gathered to give me a send-off. I got into the car, put it in gear and prepared to pull out into the road. But a surfeit of confidence tends to lead to disaster and, planning a bit of a rally start to entertain them, I pressed my foot rather too hard on the accelerator and shot off far too fast without really considering which way the wheels were facing. They were pointing straight at an ornamental rose bed in the middle of the roundabout, surrounded by lawn. I drove straight across the lawn, ploughed through the rose bed and off the other side, causing a fair bit of damage. I looked in the mirror, expecting to see horrified faces at the damage I had caused, but was greeted by the sight of the little group cheering and waving their hands. They thought it was wonderful and extremely entertaining and so did I, until I came back the next morning and was asked to sort out the ploughed field I had created.

A little while later, despite this shaky performance, I took my driving test, which I was desperate to do, as I wasn't mobile enough and bloody lazy. I took the test in my trusty baked-bean can which I'd bought off my brother for three hundred quid. It was absolutely tiny and when I saw the size of the examiner I worried that I wouldn't even be able to get him in the car, let alone drive without sitting on his lap. I took Valium, just to take the edge off my anxiety. It unfortunately made me rather too relaxed and at one point I nearly drove into a hole in the road. However, I performed a very impressive emergency stop in order to avoid it and, surprisingly, passed. My huge examiner turned out to be an ex-copper who hardly ever passed anyone, so I was extra proud.

What I really liked about this place was the whole ethos of liberalism. We had events like discos, parties and sports. I will never forget the reaction the group always had when we put on 'Thank You For the Music' by Abba. They absolutely loved it and would indulge in an orgy of stamping, singing at the tops of their voices and spinning round and round with delirious joy. Every time I hear that song an instant image in my head transports me straight back to that place and the amazing atmosphere.

One interesting dilemma we faced there involved a woman in her forties who was engaging in a rather dangerous pastime which caused some concern. She would stand out at the front of the building, which was on a main road, looking for sex from passing drivers. It wasn't just the sex that she was after, but the rewards that were forthcoming afterwards. A few local old geezers who were lonely and either widowed or single would pull up, find a convenient bush and, after the act, furnish her either with some chocolate or a packet of fags. It has to be said that she was no looker, but neither were they, and this strange contract seemed to satisfy all parties. Everyone was aware of what was going on and a staff meeting was held to discuss an action plan. To their credit, in my opinion, a decision was made to let her carry on doing it. Having weighed up the benefits and potential dangers, it was felt that it would really deplete the quality of her life, because it was the only thing she really seemed to enjoy. I can understand how distasteful this may seem to people, but I have always felt it is so unfair to exclude those with a disability, learning or physical, from the opportunity for sexual contact.

By this time I was about twenty and had packed an enormous amount into the last couple of years. I began to start thinking about the future and what I wanted to do. My mother knew that I fancied working in the arts and by that point I had considered comedy. Why did I want to do comedy? I admired comedians, even though there weren't many women stand-ups whom I could learn from. Most of the women who were famous for comedy were comedy actresses, like Beryl Reid, Joan Sims and Hattie Jacques. Women tended to fall into two categories in comedy films at the time: gorgeous and sexy and therefore the object of some leering Neanderthal's affection, or a so-called 'grotesque' – fat, ugly, nasty, a bully, a nag. Whatever exaggerated aspect of womanhood you could conceive, and none of them very pleasant.

I didn't want to be a comedy actress, though; I knew which category I'd soon enough get shunted into given half a chance. I knew that I wanted to do stand-up, compete with men and come out if not ahead of them, then at least equal. I often think that wanting to compete in such a male arena was probably to do with my brothers. Then again, plenty of women have brothers and no sisters but end up quite feminine and certainly don't want to go into comedy.

So I would hazard a guess that my mum was a major influence too, in demonstrating that women can do anything they want, not only in the way she behaved, but in her interests, the content of her conversation, her outlook on life, her politics and her wit. I think I had taken most of those on board without even realising it. Also, my dad had a nice sense of humour. In his later years it wasn't very evident but when we were younger, he mucked about, made jokes, played tricks and liked a laugh.

Other than that, I can't unravel any more overt reasons for ending up in this ridiculous job. I'm not even sure whether I was funny or quick-witted. I'd always liked telling jokes to my brothers, but is that enough? I don't think so.

My mother very sensibly pointed out to me that it would be advisable to get a qualification and/or trade under my belt before I gallivanted round the West End plying my trade, whatever that might be. So I applied for a place at Brunel University ('In Bristol? Lovely!' Um, no, in Uxbridge, near Heathrow Airport). The course I went for was known as a sandwich course (yes, I've done all the jokes). It was a four-year course, rather than the normal three years. It was called a 'Joint Social Sciences Degree' with an RMN qualification (Registered Mental Nurse – yes, done all those jokes too).

I went off to the interview and, despite the fact that it was near Uxbridge, I liked it. An added bonus was that they were prepared to take me with my very crap A-levels, which nowhere else would. So they offered me a place and I took it and got ready to start in the autumn of 1978.

There were a few loose ends to sort out before I went. Dave was one of them. We still had quite an on-off relationship. When he realised I was flying off to start a new phase in my life, he suddenly became keener. This is a common theme, I think, among uncommitted blokes, the 'Don't Know What You've Got Till It's Gone' syndrome Joni Mitchell so eloquently sang about.

By this time Dave was in Bognor Regis, but he sent me an imploring letter, asking me to join him to sort out our difficulties and get back together properly. I think the 'M' word may even have been mentioned. But the truth of it is, fond as I was of him, he was a mess, drinking heavily and generally misbehaving in a being-unfaithful-with-other-women-kind of way.

Anyway, with a trepidatious heart, just a few weeks before I was to go off to college, I set out in my little car – a Honda 600 Z Coupe, my baked-bean can on wheels – to see what we could make of the whole mess.

He'd booked a hotel room for two nights. It was adequate and had a sink right at the end of the bed, which would come in handy later on. I arrived there in the early evening, dumped my bag and we headed straight out to see what Bognor had to offer in terms of nightlife.

Not much, as it turned out. We spent quite a lot of time in various pubs and I had a very strong suspicion that he was adding something stronger to my bottle of Pils because within about half an hour, I was absolutely off my face. We ended up in a nightclub at about eleven thirty, by which time I could barely remember my own name. I found a table next to the window and halfway through our first drink there I knew I was going to throw up. I also knew I didn't have any time to make it to a handy receptacle like a toilet, so I staggered to my feet, leaned towards the window and heaved the contents of my stomach into the open air. Or so I thought. The problem was that the window wasn't open and therefore I only succeeded in decorating the glass itself with my previous meal.

Result: thrown out of the club. By this time I had

the most appalling pre-hangover headache and just wanted to lie down. But my escort wasn't finished yet and dragged my half-conscious body to a late-night bar. He sat me on a stool at the bar and went off for a piss, but no sooner had he disappeared round the corner than I keeled backwards off the stool and ended up in a heap on the floor. Result: chucked out of that bar too.

Defeat came upon us and we wandered back to the hotel, where I spent a very pleasant night kneeling at the end of the bed throwing up like a champion vomiter for hours into the very handy sink.

The next morning I thought I would be allowed to sleep, feeling as I did like I had several brain tumours and quite a few ulcers. But no, Dave was surprisingly bright and chirpy and, as the sun was streaming in through the window, suggested a stroll on the beach. I knew I could no sooner stroll than back-flip all the way down to the beach, but I dragged myself out and we managed to make it down there, whereupon I plonked myself gratefully down. Within seconds, Dave informed me he was going to find an off-licence to get a bottle of wine and wandered off. I knew if I drank any more alcohol I would die. My head was pounding, it was hot and my eyes felt as if they had been rolled in grit. So I did a really awful thing . . . I fucked off.

Making sure he wasn't heading back towards me, I legged it up the beach as fast as I could, found the car and drove off, leaving all my stuff in the hotel room and no note. The journey home was appalling, a combination of great, big, snotty sobbing and throwing up. My poor mother took one look at me and advised bed. I slept all that day and night. And that was the last time I ever saw Dave.

Chapter 13

A Spinster of the Rural Hamlet of Uxbridge

University was great. Despite my vague plans to go to Oxford or Cambridge when I was at grammar school, I'm really pleased I picked Brunel. At the time I was there, from 1978 to 1982, it had no arts department, only science and engineering, and therefore there were eight males to every female. So we tiny group of women used to joke that at least there was more chance of getting a bloke.

Brunel is situated just outside Uxbridge, and it has to be said that the area is not a charming rural hamlet by any stretch of the imagination. The university was also almost on the doorstep of Heathrow Airport and so planes went overhead very close to the ground. Eventually we just got used to it. I saw Concorde a few times but, as I am female, I wasn't that impressed by it, which I suppose is a rather shocking thing to say. It was just another metal thing up in the sky.

I wasn't very enamoured with flying. I think it's probably the feeling of lack of control. In order to counteract the sensation of rising panic in the pit of my stomach when on a plane, I used to just get pissed. Later on, when I became a comic, a friend of mine, Jeff, got me a 'Don't Be Scared of Flying' day for my birthday.

Lots of us wimps turned up at Heathrow where we were herded into a room by some official looking people. Jeff came with me and relentlessly took the piss out of each stage of our day. First of all, a pilot and a psychologist came into the room. There were about a hundred of us. He explained how planes fly, and I'm ashamed to admit that I didn't really listen so I couldn't tell you. The psychologist talked about anxiety, all of which I knew already, so I didn't listen to that either. Then we had a chance to go for a wee. Some woman in the toilet was handing out Valium to anyone who wanted it. This was not part of the service, you understand, just an enterprising member of the public. We were then taken in a bus to the terminal and walked through it in order to get on a plane which was to be flown by the same pilot who had spoken to us earlier. I got the distinct impression that all the airport staff knew exactly who we were and there were various 'looks' and tittering going on.

Finally, we mounted the steps of the plane and that's when the shenanigans started. Several people started to cry and wail and had to be physically pushed into the plane and once we sat down some people had enormous panic attacks and tried to get off. One poor woman literally tore her hair out, so terrified was she. This had rather a positive effect on me because I realised that on the scale of fear-of-flying candidates, I was a relatively mild case. Another guy gripped the arms of his seat so forcefully that his hands could not be removed from them. At one point there was a completely farcical scene reminiscent of the comedy film *Airplane*, when members of staff lined up to try to get his fists open and his hands off the seat.

Eventually the plane took off, accompanied by a serious running commentary by the pilot, during which he described every single nuance of what was happening – noises, bumps, shakes, the lot. Jeff contributed a comedy commentary and pretended he was driving a car, so as we took off he was changing gear up from first to fifth in true comedy-mime fashion. We flew down to Southampton and back and the palpable sense of relief and the enormous cheer that went up when we landed was something to behold. Some people had never even been on a plane before and there was lots of hugging and crying and other very un-British behaviour.

I would say, on the whole, it was a big help. I flew to Australia some years later and rather enjoyed it.

Brunel University itself was a very modern, higgledy-piggledy set of buildings. Rumour had it that the architect's plans for the library were misread by the builders and the library was built the wrong way round. I really hope that is true.

Also, Brunel was used as a location in the iconic film *A Clockwork Orange*, in the very first scene, when some young men kick a tramp to death. Oh, how proud we were to know that the soulless concrete buildings in which we moved and studied were used to portray the literal and moral wasteland conjured up by Stanley Kubrick.

Having no knowledge of the local area and not knowing anyone, I initially moved into halls of residence, which were full of new, scared students, most of them away from mum for the first time. Each of us was allotted a little box of a room with the absolute minimum of furniture and character. For all we knew, we could have been in a detention centre at one of the Channel ports, so sparse were our surroundings.

One story that was told time and time again was the tale of a poor unfortunate first year who went home for the weekend and returned on a Sunday night to find nothing in his room except a turfed floor and a sheep.

After a month or so in my little private hell, I decided to move out, as I could not stand the yoghurt pots with name labels on in the fridge, the queue to whip up baked beans on toast and the lack of a communal area to meet and get to know other students. Serendipitously, a fellow student a year ahead on my course wanted to move nearer the place and so we did a straightforward swap and I moved into a house-share in Ruislip and found myself sharing with three men and another woman, all on the same course as me. I loved it – the sense of separation from college, the opportunity to talk to people in the evening rather than sitting in a room staring at a minuscule black and white telly and many nights with a cheap bottle of wine, laughing our heads off.

Being mobile at university changed my life. I could drive into college, pile many pissed students into the car for nights out in London and make myself scarce when the occasion demanded it.

One of my great regrets about Brunel was the fact that The Sex Pistols played their last England gig there roughly eight weeks before I arrived. The Sex Pistols really signified something major for me and although I and most of the women I knew did a version of punk-lite, the air of rebellion and revolution that they engendered in us created an atmosphere of real anticipation that change was afoot.

Two Tone had also attracted me – bands like The Specials and Madness – and while I was at Brunel, The Specials arrived there to play. Unfortunately, a welcoming committee of skinheads, well aware of their anti-racist stance, had turned up too and before long set up a chant of '*Sieg heil*' during their first song. This was too much for Jerry Dammers, the keyboard player, who vaulted over his keyboard, grabbed a guitar and jumped off the stage, swinging it at someone's head as he did. Of course, this immediately started a massive ruck – fists and boots flew indiscriminately, security swarmed in and the gig was stopped after one song. What a pain.

We had more luck with The Damned, who were due to play a gig at the Clarendon on Hammersmith Broadway, a well-known, manky punk venue. Several of us turned up to find that the show had sold out and headed disconsolately into the downstairs bar. Spotting a door in the corner which we worked out must lead somewhere near the stage, we came up some stairs and arrived in the area where The Damned were doing a sound check. Being a punk band, they didn't give a shit that we didn't have tickets, so we watched the sound check and then got stuck in with the rest of the audience when they arrived.

I think probably the best gig that I ever went to was The Beat and The Pogues at the Hammersmith Palais. The mad, scrabbling, joyful, pissed audience bouncing up and down in a frenzied fashion, set against the loudest, most brilliant, inspiring music contributed to an evening full of huge excitement that I could not get out of my head.

My commitment to seeing bands was curtailed by lack of money and an unwillingness to leave campus. As a student in Uxbridge, travelling to the centre of London involved a long journey on the underground (we were at the end of the line) and my experience of the tube had not been pleasant, so I stopped going on it.

What put me off was an incident which occurred early one evening, when I found myself travelling into central London to meet a friend. I was in a carriage, pretty much on my own, apart from a young couple right down the other end. A guy got on and sat opposite me. I was reading a book and didn't take much notice of him. He seemed a bit fidgety but I didn't want to look at him because I had quickly learned the London tube-travel rules, which are that you don't strike up a conversation, meet anyone's eyes or get involved in any trouble. So I continued to try to read, even though it was hard to concentrate. I raised the book up a bit higher to cover my face and tried to take in the words which were swimming in front of my eyes. Then I heard the sound of a trouser zip being undone and thought to myself, 'Oh Christ, he's going to have a wank.'

The problem in these situations is that lots of us women are unsure what to do. Most of us have a vision of ourselves rising to our feet and declaiming in a loud voice, 'Stop that immediately or I will call an officer of the law!' If only. For some reason, any sort of sexually deviant behaviour disarms most women, makes them feel paralysed, frightened and ashamed, and that is what men like that rely on – that you will be too embarrassed to do anything.

I knew there was a couple down the end of the carriage, so rather than hang around for the floor show, I decided to go and seek some support. I walked up the carriage as quickly as I could and sat opposite them. They looked a bit pissed off that I had chosen to sit right by them when the carriage was empty. So, as I felt scared, embarrassed and socially awkward all at the same time, I thought I'd better explain myself. I said, 'I'm really sorry that I've had to sit here, but there's a bloke up there masturbating.' They looked at me as if I was mad and got up and walked away to the next carriage.

Cheers, guys, thanks for your help. I suppose this is the concern of a lot of people in London: that the have-a-go hero will always get it in the neck and therefore you must at all costs keep out of trouble. But this incident made me angry and I resolved to try in future to be a good citizen who got stuck in, whatever the risk.

I got the opportunity a year or so later, when I was in Camden Market, a bustling student paradise with everything the aspiring fashionista could want to buy reasonably cheaply. I had decided to have a mooch around on my own and meet a friend later. It was raining and the streets were very crowded. As I walked along I became aware of a couple in their thirties arguing. The man was about six foot and very well built, whereas the woman was much smaller and thinner, and he towered over her. Initially, he had just been shouting at her, but then he started to get more threatening and push her around a bit. This all happened in seconds and, as I passed, he began to raise his fist. Many other people had noticed it going on and were studiously avoiding looking at it. It started to rain more heavily. I just could not ignore it, so I walked up to them and shouted at the bloke, 'What the fuck do you think you're doing?'

He was obviously totally shocked that I had intervened and turned to look at me with an expression that said, 'And who the fuck are you?'

The woman seized her chance. She had been holding a rolled-up umbrella and she raised it as high as she could and brought it down on his head with a huge thwack. Neither she nor I stayed around to face the consequences. We both legged it in opposite directions and disappeared into the crowd.

So, the upshot of those kinds of incidents was that I generally stayed on campus to watch what the entertainments manager had cobbled together as some sort of varied music programme.

I saw Hazel O'Connor, a punk-ish singer with a shock of bright-blond hair, who was quite famous at the time with two singles in the charts, 'Will You' and 'Eighth Day'. She also had a hit film out, *Breaking Glass*, which I went to see. There was a splendid old-fashioned commissionaire outside – uniform, braided cap and all – shouting very entertainingly, 'This way for *Broken Glass*!' During the film, Hazel O'Connor's character takes an overdose and there is a scene in which she very dozily tries to come round. Some wag in the cinema shouted, 'Wake up, love, for fuck's sake, we're bored shitless.' It got the biggest reaction of the night.

On our occasional ventures to the cinema in Uxbridge, it was slightly frightening, because the place tended to be patrolled by packs of young lads at night. One time we went to see *Straw Dogs*, a very violent film set in the West Country and directed by Sam Peckinpah. There is a legendary rape scene in which the female star, Susan George, is attacked by some local Neanderthals and begins to enjoy it halfway through. Loads of women, including us, got up and walked out during this scene. I was very impressed by this protest. I think you'll find women enjoying rape is a purely male fantasy.

I also saw The Vapors while at Brunel. They were

one-hit wonders with their single 'Turning Japanese', which is apparently about masturbation. Yes, work it out. Then there was Paul Young and a hideous Radio One roadshow with Dave Lee Travis, who rose up on to the stage dressed in a silver robot costume. Unintentionally very funny.

This was as close as I got to DLT sadly, but I did have a couple of exciting celeb encounters in the early eighties. My friend Betty and I knew some cool people who organised parties in central London and one night we were invited to a warehouse party to launch Debbie Harry's new film, *Videodrome*. We had a whale of a time, got very pissed and stood next to Debbie Harry for a while. She was rather overweight at the time, having been ill I think, and we could not believe our thighs were smaller than hers. We fell asleep on the night bus and ended up somewhere like Harlesden and had to walk home in the freezing cold, stopping to examine a cat on the pavement which seemed to have frozen solid, a rictus grin on its face.

One day we overstretched ourselves in terms of a cultural expedition. We decided to drive down to Exeter to see the first night of Anthony Minghella's play, *Two Planks and a Passion*. One of my three best friends, Edana, is Anthony's sister and we were all very excited that we knew someone who was becoming famous.

We drove down in Edana's tired old yellow Renault. Exeter is a bloody long way from Uxbridge. The play was magnificent, like a medieval mummers' play. After the performance, we went for dinner and met Anthony, a charming, impressive man, very gracious and fiercely intelligent. The enormous tragedy of his early death dealt a very powerful blow to his absolutely delightful family, and many others.

After seeing the play, we had to drive home and it was absolutely pissing with rain. I'd agreed to drive back and everyone else in the car dropped off to sleep. At the time, the M4 was blessed with a number of deep grooves which, in the wet weather, used to fill with water and become small ponds. I hit one of these at about seventy miles an hour, and the car aquaplaned across the road towards the central reservation. I remember thinking, 'Christ, I'm going to kill them all and they won't even know about it.' Thank God, the car came out of the skid just as we were about to hit the central barrier and I managed to straighten it up. Everyone else snoozed on and I cried with relief, feeling very alone in the pouring rain somewhere near Swindon.

Anyway, back to Brunel. While at university, I had some cracking holidays on a shoestring, because as students that was all we could run to. I went to Greece a few times with various combinations of friends. We went to Skopelos, Skiathos, Crete and Ios.

In Ios I met a very nice soldier who was a conscript and didn't want to be a soldier at all. We spent a lovely night on the beach together, talking bollocks, snogging and trying to communicate in his very bad English and my even worse Greek. As the sun began to rise, he realised that he was late getting back to the barracks and ran off up the beach, shouting that he would meet me the following night at the same place. He never turned up and I was mighty miffed. After a few days, I received a message that because he had been late back to barracks, he had been confined there for a fortnight as a punishment. And that worked out at two days after the day I left. The course of true love, blah, blah.

I went to Crete with Lizzie, who was a true free spirit, and within a day she had met a toothless hippie, formed a huge attachment to him and gone to live on the beach with him, leaving me to my own devices in our little rented cottage. I got to know a few people and spent my days on the beach, but the nights were hell. This was because the middle-aged Greek man who owned the row of cottages had taken a fancy to me and each night he would come round at midnight and try to talk his way in for a bit of copulation. Most evenings he was quite easily persuaded to go away, but one night he came round really drunk, accompanied by a huge Alsatian, and started banging on the door and kicking it to try to break it down. It was terrifying. I pushed all the furniture up against the door and sat on my bed. He gave up after about half an hour and I sat there until the morning. I packed all our stuff, hauled it down to the beach to find Lizzie and told her we had to get out of town. She grudgingly bade goodbye to Mr Toothless Hippie and, as we had no money, we went down to the local bank. But someone had been there first. The bank manager was none other than the brother of the amorous psycho who had tried to batter my door down. He refused to give us any money, so we were forced to start walking until a kind old farmer agreed to give us a lift and dropped us off in the next town.

Of course, along with all the social happiness that university offered, there was the small matter of getting a degree. My attitude to studying, I'm afraid, has always had an element of the 'fuck it, that'll do' to it. That's not to say I didn't enjoy it, because a lot of it was fascinating. Each year we took three subjects, which we could choose from a list of about nine.

One could never tell how interesting the course was going to be, or how good the lecturer was. You just had to hope. We also had to do a statistics course and take an exam at the end of it. This was an open exam that you were allowed to take books and old exam papers into. I got hold of some old papers from a friend, and when I went into the exam I discovered about seventy per cent of the questions were exactly the same and she'd got them all right, so I just copied them. I prefer to think of that as resourceful rather than cheating.

Let's say, I got by. Party or work? I knew which one I would always go for. I chose courses on the basis of whether they sounded a laugh or not and therefore ended up doing an odd mixture of the sublime and the ridiculous. I chose evolutionary psychology and ethnomethodology one year. Evolutionary psychology was fascinating and taught me a lot about the way gene pools behave, 'a mixture of radical change and pragmatic conservatism', a phrase that has stuck in my head for years. I remember once saying to our professor, 'Do you think there could ever be a sexually transmitted disease that actually kills people?' He seemed dubious, but about a year later HIV and AIDS seared themselves into our consciousness. It was perhaps the only intelligent observation I ever made at university. I asked this question because at the time we were covering disease transmission and it just occurred to me that no sexually transmitted diseases were fatal. At the time.

Ethnomethodology, on the other hand, was bonkers, a branch of sociology that examined the minutiae of everyday social encounters by reducing them to the tiniest slivers of interaction by turning them on their head to reveal the paradoxes at the heart of the way we relate to each other. It meant that we indulged in a number of surreal social experiments around the streets of Uxbridge, whose residents didn't seem ready for us at all.

For example, we had to go out on the streets and ask random individuals the way somewhere, but pretend each time they refined their explanation that we simply didn't understand their directions. The poor bloke I asked ended up saying, 'For fuck's sake, are you foreign or something?' and walked off, while another woman's direction-giver got so frustrated that he actually put her in his car and drove her to where she wanted to go.

One experiment which revealed so much about the way we interpret things was carried out with a group of students who were invited to ask questions about any aspect of their lives. Some were given random answers generated by a computer and others were advised by a professional counsellor. Of course, both groups confessed themselves completely satisfied with the answers they were given, which just goes to show that we are all completely suggestible.

I got into trouble academically on a couple of occasions. Once, when I was under pressure to turn an essay in, I copied the essay of a friend who'd got an A grade for it, so felt smugly confident that I could get it through. I was excessively despondent when I received it back with a C minus and was chided for something that was 'well out of character' compared to my customary offerings.

Another time, when I was in a hurry, I copied chunks out of an obscure book. I can remember almost verbatim what my tutor wrote at the end: 'On first reading I believed this to be an excellent piece of work.' So far, so good. 'But on re-reading, it dawned on me that you have actually copied numerous, enormous paragraphs word for word from a text not often used in the present day. Please arrange to see me.' (Why do they have to be such clever bastards?) I did go and see him and he gave me a mini lecture about plagiarism and said things like 'You are far too clever to be doing this sort of thing.' It had the required effect. I never did that again.

Still, I was managing to get through without falling too far behind. So this gave me time for fun. A friend and I became involved in Brunel Radio and had a show answering student problems in a comedy way. We were given far more leeway than Radio Two allowed Jonathan Ross and Russell Brand, and found ourselves getting ruder and ruder, until we were gently sacked.

One problem at university was money. During one six-month period of each year we were paid as student nurses, so could just about get by, but for the rest of the year, things were tight. This led to some very dull jobs just to supplement my income, perhaps the worst being a barmaid in a trucker's pub in Uxbridge. And, God, was it grim. I remember one night a huge and hideous trucker arriving at the bar and pulling up his grimy vest to reveal a tattoo of a naked woman with her legs wide open on his fulsome stomach. He virtually pulled my head off trying to drag me over the bar to get a closer look, with the words, 'What do you think of that, love?' I didn't think of anything funny to say at the time but, as with many incidents in my life, it was eventually worked into a comedy routine.

Parties became wilder and behaviour more extreme. Everyone knows the delicious disinhibiting effect alcohol has on us all. It makes you do things like play truth or dare. One night I lost and was instructed to go and knock on a random door and when the inhabitant of the flat answered, I was to shout, 'Afghanistan Bananistan!' at the top of my voice and leg it. As instructed, I picked a random door (it was two o' clock in the morning by now) and waited giggling for a grumpy, knackered student to answer. Unfortunately, the door was opened by the elderly mother of a student, whom she'd come to visit for the weekend. Her dressing gown was a vision of pink nylon and she even had her curlers in.

Still, not one to shy away from a dare, I chanted my pathetic phrase, which of course was related to the Russian invasion at the time, and ran off as quickly as I could, feeling slightly ashamed despite my drunkenness.

At another party, someone set off the fire alarm. In due course, the fire brigade turned up. It was a fancy-dress party. I was in my little room in halls, which I'd moved back to for the third year. There was a huge banging on the door and someone was shouting, 'Fire brigade!' I opened the door and made the assumption that this was brilliant fancy dress. 'Well done, mate,' I said, 'good effort,' and slammed the door, whereupon he promptly kicked it in, convincing me finally that he was a bona fide fireman.

The accommodation on offer to students is unsavoury to say the least. Lack of funds dictates that it will either be a swamp, a hovel or a hard-to-let nightmare. In 1980, we found a reasonably nice place above a fish and chip shop (oh joy) in West Drayton (oh horror) owned by a lovely extended Asian family. The one draw-back was that the patriarch requested we make our sitting-room floor available every weekend for his twenty-one-year-old son to sleep on in a camp bed. As we were three women and a gay bloke, we didn't feel very comfortable about this arrangement and a stand-off occurred which nearly lost us the flat, but eventually dad caved in. However, this did not stop the family from turning up unannounced en masse from time to time, to sit in our kitchen and drink tea. As we were students and sometimes didn't get up till *Countdown* came on at half four, we would arrive in the kitchen to find a huge group of sari-clad middle-aged women nattering away quite happily and eating our biscuits.

But we didn't mind because we lived above a chip shop.

One of those questions that is often asked is 'Do you remember where you were when [fill in the blank] died?'

Well, I remember very well where I was when John Lennon was shot on 8 December 1980. Living above a chip shop in West Drayton. We'd all come home from college and were lying around in various states of exhaustion, having done absolutely bugger all that day again. The news came on and the first item was very difficult to believe: John Lennon had been shot outside his apartment in New York. These surreal moments are difficult to fit into the run-of-the-mill progress of one's life. Lennon was always my favourite Beatle, despite the reputation he had for being difficult and arsey. He seemed to be the one who had extricated himself from the swamp of pop celebrity and gone his own way.

These sorts of incidents, the ending of someone's life at too young an age – and I realise what a cliché it is to say this – tend to crystallise one's attitude towards the unthinking plodding of one's existence. The fragility of one's presence on the planet is something most of us prefer not to address, so it is a relief when the blinkers come down again and one is distracted by a soap opera or a banal problem and settles back into a state of blissfully ignoring one's mortality. '*Carpe diem*' and all those other exhortations to change the course of one's life, to introduce a sense of urgency and excitement, don't really work on humans unless they exist in a constant state of desperation, like during a war. We smug and comfortable types in the West simply don't seem to be able to get the balance right. In fact, I suspect most of us actively avoid it.

So, on the academic side, I suppose I continued to plod. I stood for president of the Students' Union for a laugh, and it served me right that I only got eight votes, because I didn't have a campaign, couldn't be bothered to put up a poster and had not a single policy to speak of. Lord knows what would have happened if I'd actually been voted in. I would have run a mile, I suspect.

Ah, happy days! Though having said that, entries in my diary – which only appeared when I was depressed, because when I was happy I was too busy to say so – seem to gainsay what my memories are. For example: 'Brunel is absolutely horrible at the moment. Can't muster any enthusiasm to do any work.' And 'Boring day. Only thing I did was some washing.'

There seem to have been quite a few days like this. So much for '*carpe diem*'.

Chapter 14

Ooh, Matron!

Doing a so-called 'sandwich course' is for some an unsettling existence, as at regular intervals you move from one arena to another and are expected to just get on with it. For me, though, it was perfect. As a kid we'd moved house a lot, so I was used to the constant changing of an address and a life and it seemed familiar to me.

So each spring we would pack up our meagre student belongings and head to Camberwell, in the heart of south-east London.

Most of us, having lost the will to find any accommodation, would settle into the nurses' homes, either in Camberwell at the Maudsley Hospital or in a slightly more leafy area seven miles away, West Wickham, where the Bethlem Royal Hospital, Maudsley's sister hospital, was located. This got its name from the original Bedlam Hospital, famously known for its entertainment opportunities, as the general public were allowed to wander round for a small fee and look at 'the loonies'. Obviously we are more sophisticated these days and watch them on television, in shows like *Big Brother*.

The aim was that we would qualify as psychiatric nurses or RMNs after four years of training. Normally this training would involve a three-month placement at a general hospital, learning to do all those medical things that even as a psychiatric nurse you are required to do, like give injections, take blood pressures and administer medicine. However, the powers that be felt that we degree nurses were way too clever to spend three months on this sort of placement and it was assumed that we could learn it all by practising on a dummy in the school of nursing. This was their first mistake.

My first ward was a general psychiatry ward set in the rural gorgeousness of the Bethlem Royal Hospital. The ward had roughly twenty beds and the residents were a mixture of people of all ages and with most conceivable psychiatric illnesses, ranging from depression, anxiety and anorexia to schizophrenia and manic depression (now known as 'bipolar disorder' in hideous American lingo).

Care of patients was organised into four main phases.

Assessment

This would happen as soon as someone was admitted and was a combination of observation by nurses and interviews with doctors, who would do something called a mental-state examination to try to work out what was wrong with the individual. So, for example, someone with depression would be asked about their thoughts (perhaps questioned as to whether they had any intention of killing themselves), their daily life and the aspects of it that may have been affected by depression, such as their sleeping patterns or eating habits. Nurses would observe patients and note down signs of depression, such as weight loss.

For psychotic illnesses like schizophrenia, doctors would need to find out whether the person had Schneider's first-rank symptoms, as we called them at the time. These are not used anymore and psychiatry has moved on to a slightly more sophisticated assessment of symptoms. We would be looking for whether they were hearing voices, if they had delusions – maybe paranoid or grandiose – basically anything that fitted into the typical pattern of their illness.

Treatment

On the basis of these observations, a treatment plan would be decided upon. This would often involve a drug prescription, counselling or occupational therapy, depending on what was deemed appropriate.

I think it's important here to address that fantasised-about and much-derided treatment, ECT or electro-convulsive therapy, so beloved of films about psychiatric patients. As nurses we were expected to assist with ECT.

First, we would take them from the ward down to the room where it was to be administered. What ECT does is induce a pseudo epileptic fit, because, put simply, some Italian doctor noticed many years ago that lots of epileptics were a lot more cheerful after they'd had a fit. An epileptic fit is an excess of electrical activity in the brain, an overload, if you like.

So the patient would be put to sleep with an anaesthetic and two paddles attached to a machine were held to their head. The paddles were like those things they use in casualty for people who have had heart attacks, except smaller and rounder. An electric shock would then be delivered, the individual would convulse briefly – i.e. have a fit – and then they would lie on the bed for a while until they came round from the anaesthetic.

As far as I can remember, in the film *One Flew Over the Cuckoo's Nest*, an iconic and brilliant movie, the main character, Randle Patrick McMurphy, played by Jack Nicholson, is given ECT without anaesthetic as a punishment. This is certainly not the case in real life, although there has been much criticism of the use of ECT. My opinion is that this is because it is used too widely, on inappropriate forms of depression. There are side effects, such as loss of short-term memory, and these are a major part of the controversy. It seems to me, though, that when used on a very particular form of agitated depression, it can have remarkable results.

When I was a student, we had a woman admitted with the worst case of agitated depression I have ever seen. She cried out constantly, could not sit still, wandered round the ward all day wringing her hands and clutching at her face and clothes, and was so completely overwrought with emotion, desperate and sad, that it was painful to witness. This woman had about five sessions of ECT and the transformation in her was absolutely unbelievable. She became calm, articulate, relaxed, friendly, communicative and her mood was happy and contented. I could not believe what I was seeing. On the other hand, I witnessed many patients who were given ECT, on whom it had no effect whatsoever.

Once assessments were done, it was up to the nursing staff, as I said, to administer the treatment and sometimes, for those people who were seriously disturbed and had no insight into their illnesses, their treatment was unwelcome to them. So this would involve giving it to them forcibly. This was always meticulously planned and executed, so that no one, most of all the patient, was in any danger. It is not a pleasant thing to do and no one enjoyed doing it, but the future welfare of the individual was always uppermost and I did it for no reason other than that. We were permitted to do this because the individuals had been sectioned under the Mental Health Act and, although I'm aware that there is the potential for abuse in these circumstances, I very rarely felt uncomfortable in what I was doing.

Manic depression, or bipolar disorder, is an illness that can be well controlled by a specific drug. This is not without long-term side effects, though, and I felt so sorry for those who had to be on the drug for the rest of their lives. Many of those with bipolar disorder become well through taking the drug, but if they stopped taking it, the whole circular process would start again.

Discharge

Once someone was considered to be well enough to go home – and I have to say that in many cases this was a fluid concept because some people never fully recovered and never would because they had chronic, incurable illnesses that could only be managed – it was arranged for them to leave. As nurses, we would make sure their drugs were given to them and help them pack their things up. Most of the time it was a happy occasion, although sometimes you knew you would see them again in a few months when they defaulted on their medication.

Follow-up

Mostly patients would attend regular outpatients' appointments so the doctors could check how they were doing. Very occasionally they would come back to the ward to visit a nurse for an ongoing assessment. And the other option was for them to be followed-up in their home by a community psychiatric nurse.

*   *   *

The staff on the ward were a mixture of very capable and absolutely bloody useless. One particular nurse had probably been in the job too long and could not resist teasing the patients. On the ward was an anorexic woman in her late sixties (which is very unusual) and each time a plane flew overhead, this nurse would look at the sky and say, 'Here comes your weekly consignment of sausages.'

This very thin woman was the first person I was ever let loose on with a syringe, after the sister instructed me to give her an injection – my first piercing of a real human being. As she weighed approximately five and a half stone, this worried me enormously. Armed only with knowledge gleaned from practising on an orange in the school of nursing, I approached her with trepidation. We had been told that we had to inject people in the 'upper outer quadrant' of their buttock, and if we put the needle in the wrong place, we could potentially paralyse someone for life. Great.

But a person who weighs little more than five stone doesn't actually have a buttock, so, poor woman, I had to get her to lie on her side and then I gathered up as much loose skin as I could to form a pseudo bum cheek. Then, virtually with my eyes closed and my heart pounding, I bunged the syringe into her bum and delivered the liquid.

I was sure I'd got it in the wrong place and was forced to follow her round for the rest of the shift to make sure she wasn't paralysed. Even after I went off duty, I found an excuse to ring the ward, dropped her casually into the conversation and heard, with relief, that she was still walking around and hadn't keeled over.

Being rubbish at the physical side of nursing was a constant theme throughout my training and nursing career. I ran like the wind in the other direction whenever there was an emergency like a cardiac arrest, and I was constantly trying to avoid giving injections or taking blood pressures. However, taking blood pressures is quite a feature of psychiatric nursing and it was hard to sidestep. Put the cuff on the arm, inflate it and place the end of the stethoscope in the crook of the arm and listen while the cuff deflates. The top figure of a blood pressure measure is taken when the 'boom boom' noise starts and the lower measurement is taken when it stops. Problem was, half the time I couldn't hear a bloody thing. And I felt it wasn't polite to try to take the readings more than five times. So, I'm ashamed to say, most of the time when I was cornered and had tried my best with no success, I looked at the chart and made up a figure that was similar to the last measurement. Yes, I know it's a terrible, shameful and downright dangerous thing to do, but I tried always to compensate either by keeping an eye on them or surreptitiously persuading someone else to do it the next time it was due.

Ditto, injections. I found these an ordeal and I remember that once I had to inject a thick, glutinous substance into some poor woman's buttock and just found it impossible to get in. After several attempts, the unfortunate woman turned to me and said, 'Can I just take a tablet?'

Later on, after I had qualified, a situation arose in which I was required to give a very disturbed woman a forced injection while several people held her still. In a slight state of panic, I pressed the plunger in too quickly and, as I pulled it out, the entire contents of the syringe squirted out of the pinprick-sized hole in her bum and hit me in the face. All I could hear was six people sniggering.

Perhaps the biggest drama I experienced on my first ward was on one of my compulsory stretches of night duty. The main thing about nights was that unless you had someone on the ward who was hypomanic (the high end of bipolar) most people slept all the way through, leaving long, uneventful stretches with the other nurse who partnered you at one end of the ward.

I wish this particular night had been uneventful really, because that would have been preferable. I was partnered with a male nurse who obviously saw young students as fair game, and each night his conversation would be laced with dirty jokes, unsavoury suggestions and requests to meet up outside work. Suffice it to say, he wasn't my type, and I began to long for my block of nights to be over, as it was intolerable. I was ambivalent about whether to report him, as it was a grey area and he never stepped over the mark (or at least he could have argued that he hadn't). On the final night he was even more frisky than usual and endlessly harassed me whenever we were on our own. I'd made it perfectly clear, in as polite a way as possible, that I wasn't interested, and I was nearing the end of my tether. He, on the other hand, seemed to be a combination of enormously frustrated by my rejection of him and quite excited. We were sitting a few feet from each other when he leaned towards me and said (and how could I forget these words of love?), 'It's like seeing a piece of meat in a butcher's window that you can't afford.' Then he half threw himself at me and half just fell over on top of me, trapping me in my chair.

Well, what do you do? You're in a mental hospital in the middle of the night and a colleague is rubbing himself up and down you. I shouted, 'Help!'

Almost immediately, two patients – a depressed woman and a man with anxiety – appeared from their rooms and as soon as he became aware of their presence, he immediately pulled back from our surreal embrace and sat in his chair as if nothing had happened. I, however, was slightly shocked and found myself being comforted by two people I was supposed to be looking after.

'You should report him,' the woman said.

I didn't. Should I have done? Maybe. But I was too new, too unsure of myself and the matter was never mentioned again.

I'm aware I'm making myself sound like some ridiculously sultry beauty that men can't resist. But, although I wasn't unattractive, I still wasn't your traditional idea of a gorgeous lady. It just goes to show that looks are not that important to pervy men, I suppose.

After doing general psychiatry, I then specialised in different psychiatric disciplines for two years. I did a few months on a ward for the elderly, which I found heartbreaking. At the time, an experiment involving a new drug for dementia was being carried out on the ward and an unfortunate side effect was that it made those who took it smell very strongly of fish. So not only were the poor old buggers struggling to communicate, but also no one wanted to go near them. On this placement, we also did visits in the community and I had been assigned a woman in Peckham to spend some time with. I was supposed to assess how she was coping at home. When I was dropped off by the lovely minibus driver in front of her shabby prefab, I felt apprehensive, as it was my first home assessment. I knew she was suffering from a schizophrenic illness in which paranoia was a feature, but I made the mistake of thinking, 'Ah, she'll be a nice old lady. We'll drink tea and have Rich Tea biscuits and it'll all be fine.'

But no. The minute I got through the door, I could tell she really wasn't in good shape mentally. Added to that, she was a big, sturdy, south London woman, tough as old boots. And she appeared very, very paranoid indeed. She shoved me away from the door and started to push a pretty hefty chest of drawers up against it. Part of me wanted to laugh, so strange was this whole situation. But I retained a professional demeanour and gently remonstrated with her, while attempting to wrestle the chest of drawers off her and push it back to its original position. Without any warning, she gave me a hell of a whack in the shoulder and, bloody hell, did it hurt. It took me totally by surprise and I just didn't know what to do. She was muttering under her breath, mostly stuff I couldn't understand, but she managed to make it perfectly clear that if I intervened again, I would get more of the same. So what to do? My first instinct was to leave and get some help, but every time I tried to get near the door, she whacked me again. After a couple of pretty hard punches, I gave up on that idea and resigned myself to trying to strike up a conversation and keep away from her fists.

Six hours later, I was still pretty much in the same position. All my clever escape ruses had been foiled (all right then, there weren't any). I had to sit tight and wait for my knight in shining minibus. He arrived right on time and knocked at the door and I managed to shout that I was trapped and she wouldn't let me out. Eventually he managed to force his way in, but not before she'd had a couple more pops at me. I emerged with him, blinking in the afternoon sunlight, battered, confused and extraordinarily embarrassed by being trapped in a house and battered by a seventy-nine-year-old woman.

So, my life on a ward for the elderly: more exciting than I'd assumed.

My next stint of training involved a period on the adolescent unit at the Bethlem Royal Hospital, and that was not easy either. There were many anorexic girls, who would go to enormous lengths to hide the food that they didn't want to eat. In suitcases, under beds, in wardrobes, in piles of clothes, in plant pots. In fact, everywhere you looked there was unwanted food. For someone who loved their food and had always been taught that it was a sin to waste it, these few months were unpalatable in so many ways.

I felt sorry for most of the people in the unit. Adolescence is such a hideous time anyway, let alone when you have a mental illness tacked on top of the hormonal rumblings, hypersensitivity and doubts about whether you are going to fit into the world. In some ways, I was glad to move on.

We spent a day a week in the school of nursing throughout the training period, and the array of teaching staff was a glory to behold. From tight-lipped and snooty through to humorous and delightful, they attempted to knock us into shape, with some difficulty at times.

One lovely teacher was an innocent, who perhaps shouldn't have been allowed out in the real world. One day, while we were discussing a ward which contained quite a number of dangerous forensic patients, she advised us to avoid the place if we possibly could.

'Why's that?' we asked.

'Because there's a lot of budgery goes on up there,' was her straight-faced reply. We laughed a lot afterwards.

Speaking of 'budgery', the nurses' home attracted some unsavoury characters, inside and out. The 'Carry On' reputation of nurses' homes is well deserved to some extent and there were few who did not take advantage of the supply of nurses on tap. Of course, there are far more men in psychiatric nursing than general nursing, so it's reasonably even. And then, of course, there are doctors. I steered clear of doctors on the whole, apart from a few encounters. I remember once having what I suppose you'd call a date at the local pub. Not very relaxing, as a few of the patients from the long-term unit of the Maudsley would come in and occasionally wreak havoc. The speciality of one was to run in and do a sort of SAS assault course of drinking everyone's pints in one gulp. By the time anyone was stirred into action and tried to grab him, he was long gone.

Back to my so-called date, a sweet little doctor, who at some point during the evening turned to me and said, 'I want to see you again, when Cassiopeia is in the ascendant.' Twat. Never saw him again.

I had a few scary encounters in the environs of the nurses' home. One night I was in my car, just pulling out of the car park. It was getting dark and a man approached me and tapped on the window. Unthinkingly, because most of us don't have our pervert radar on 24/7, I wound down the window, at which point he stuck his penis in through it, heading for my face.

Everyone asks, 'Did you wind the window up?' Well, I tried, but in those days I had a cheap little car with manual windows and it seemed much easier to roar off, leaving him there shouting abuse and wondering what to do with his erection.

One night, after a fairly mad party, I was in my little room and, hard as I tried, I could not shake off the feeling that there was someone outside my door. I've no idea why. There was no noise at all; it was just a very strong sense. The feeling got stronger and stronger and, despite the fact that I always scream at the screen when women in horror films decide to go into battle with psycho killers bearing only a pair of nail clippers, I just had to look to reassure myself that my instinct was wrong.

I opened my door to discover a man standing staring into my room, his face about three inches from mine. I screamed, shut the door and barricaded myself in. I think I was the only one in that night, which made it even more terrifying. So I sat on my bed, clutching my knees, and listened to him smash up anything available for smashing – not much to be honest, a sad old pot plant and a phone in the hall. I don't think I slept until it got light. And no, we never found out who it was.

I remember a friend of mine, who was a nurse, telling me that she got into bed one night, read a magazine and then put it down on the floor, as she was tired. As she leaned across to turn off the bedside light, she saw the magazine slide under the bed. What would you do?

Well, the door was at the end of the bed, so she stood up, ran along the bed, took an almighty leap off it and got out of the room before whoever it was grabbed her. He escaped out of the window and was never found either.

Throughout much of my training I was going out with Ian, a nursing assistant on the learning-disability unit. He was a really good laugh. On our first date we went to see *The Great Rock 'n' Roll Swindle* and then had Kentucky Fried Chicken afterwards. It was bloody great. Ian loved a drink and a dance and would always get stuck right in the middle of a pogoing sesh if we went to see a band. Inevitably he would break his glasses and they were covered in Sellotape and plasters most of the time.

We lived together for a bit and he would frequently head off to town to meet his friends, a motley crew known as 'the Family'. One night he came back, off his face, at about three in the morning, and stumbled into our bedroom followed by a cab driver, who was obviously terrified he wasn't going to get paid. Funnily enough, I wasn't too happy about that.

One year Ian asked me if I would come on a working holiday with him to Butlin's on Hayling Island, as they were short of staff. We had a great week, even though it was hard work, as a lot of the kids were severely disabled and one or two had to be held all the time.

In many ways it was just like a normal Butlin's holiday. We went to the beach, attended discos and ate mountains of chips. The fact that we had many seriously disabled kids to look after was the only difference. There were little chalets where staff slept in rooms next door to the kids. It was a very joyful holiday. The kids were hugely excited, and so were we.

While I was there, I made friends with two fourteen-year-old boys with Down's syndrome. One day, one of the boys got very jealous of the other, whom he seemed to think I was favouring. Off he went to a member of staff and told them that I had been 'fiddling' with him in the bushes to get me back for favouring his friend. Thank God, the staff member had a word with me privately and said that he had done this before.

After the adolescent ward and the ward for the elderly, I worked on the drug unit and the locked ward for those at risk to others or themselves.

The drug unit was a bit depressing and slightly too close to home. What I found weird about it was that all the 'patients' were young men and women of a similar age to me, who had no identifiable 'illness' as such. They would come in for roughly six months and, on the whole, were put on methadone, a heroin substitute, the amount of which would gradually be reduced. Hand in hand with this there would be group therapy sessions in which they would all talk about their addictions and their hopes for the future. The main problem was when they got back home and dived straight back into their old social lives, which involved drugs.

I'm afraid the success rate wasn't great, and we always used to say that more patients there got off with staff than off drugs. The staff were roughly the same age as the addicts, most of whom were charming and personable, and it was difficult at times to maintain a professional distance. One had to bear in mind, though, that many addicts are very manipulative people who would do anything to get some drugs. It was not unheard of for nurses to end up having relationships with drug-unit patients, and indeed a few nurses left the unit and moved in with patients.

This was not a problem on the locked ward, however, where the vast majority of the people we cared for were very disturbed and occasionally very dangerous. A typical incident involved a well-known actor who had been brought in by the police, having been found hanging from the ledge of his bedroom window. He was in the manic phase of bipolar disorder and was very disinhibited and emotionally labile. Every morning we would attempt to have a group session, not always easy when people are so ill. I will never forget the scene one day: an unkempt gang of patients sitting round while one huge, naked man lay on the floor with matches between each of his toes chanting, and the actor jumping on to a chair and trying to lead everyone in a chorus of 'Oh, What a Beautiful Morning'.

They didn't join in.

The whole issue of violence in psychiatric hospitals is tricky. I firmly believe that incidents of aggression can be kept to a minimum if you have good nurses who are well trained. Rising tension can be nipped in the bud and any flare-up handled with the minimum of injury if nurses work as a team and know what they are doing. Also, once you know someone very well, it is so much easier to pinpoint their boiling point. One has to understand that a lot of people who go through psychiatric hospitals are very frightened and don't understand what is going on and therefore the way you treat them is so important in terms of gaining trust and building a relationship. Right, that's the lecture over.

My final ward was a general psychiatry one which specialised in disorders like epilepsy. By this time I was nearly qualified and was often put in charge of the ward on my own, a pretty stressful situation the first few times. Thankfully, I never made any massive faux pas and passed my final nursing exam. At Brunel, I got a 2:1 social sciences degree and I thought I was likely to get some high-flying research job in telly. Little did I know.

Chapter 15

Actress, TV Researcher or Nurse?

In 1982 I rather hoped that, armed with my degree, I could rule the world. So, while still at college, I scanned the media pages of the *Guardian* and decided that surely I would be needed in the world of television. I couldn't really find much that was appropriate, apart from an ad for a series on racism, for which they were looking for researchers.

The whole area of race had always interested me and, having worked in a multicultural area for so long, I was still surprised and shocked by dinosaur-like attitudes. A metamorphosis had been taking place for quite some years, which saw us as a society moving from purely white to mixed-race, and the second generation of Afro-Caribbeans and Asians were establishing themselves. Many of the older generation, including my dad, still seemed to be mired in old attitudes, but the genesis and rise of, for example, the alternative comedy scene addressed political issues like race and gender, and I wanted to be part of it.

Although I was aware of it and it sounded like my cup of tea, I didn't actually get involved until some years later. The first wave of comics who worked at the Comedy Store included Dawn French and Jennifer Saunders, Alexei Sayle, Rick Mayall and Ade Edmondson, Jenny Lecoat and many others. I didn't go and see comedy at that point. I don't know whether I thought I would feel too envious that they were doing it and I wasn't, or whether I would be intimidated by it and it would put me off trying to do it. I had a vision of myself on a stage doing stand-up and, I suppose, I feared that any interposing of real life might push that fantasy further away.

I applied for the research job at Channel 4. I think they had specified that they were looking for individuals from different ethnic backgrounds, but I ignored this, reasoning that it was important for there to be at least a few white people on board.

I was actually interviewed by Trevor Phillips, now head of the Commission for Racial Equality. The interview went all right and I awaited the outcome with a reasonably optimistic heart. Of course, it wasn't good news and I didn't get the job – what did they want with a stout white woman with no experience? I have always had the ability to move on and look forward, so I did.

I had it in my head that I'd like to have a bash at stand-up. Apart from the lifestyle of the comic, which I thought would be amazing, I assumed the hours would be good. After all, surely it would just involve going to a gig, doing your half an hour and going home. What could be better than that? Compared to nursing, it would surely be a piece of piss. At the time I couldn't really connect comedy and nursing, but, looking back now, I realise that the amount of verbal abuse I got as a nurse and the way that I had learned to let it wash over me (mostly), set me up as a bit of a tough old bird able to deal with hecklers.

I have to hand it to them, psychiatric patients are much better at heckling than audiences are. There is something about them that enables them to twist the knife once they've pushed it in, and I felt that if I could withstand the onslaught of drunks, schizophrenics and misogynistic men with personality disorders, surely I could cope with the verbal abuse that was coming my way.

For me, the personal rewards that come with doing stand-up are huge. I think it's a natural human instinct to want people to concur with your world view, even against their better judgement. Added to that, we all like to be able to elicit a laugh. Humour is so important. It knits people together, it disperses tension, it sets up a delicious us-against-them mentality and it gives people a great night out. We all know that laughing releases chemicals in the body that improve our well-being and make us happy, and there is nothing quite like standing in front of a crowd of people whom you have made laugh. To me it is not really about the 'high' that many comics describe; it's more a feeling of intense satisfaction that you have clocked up another victory and connected with people. And the more scary the gig, the greater the satisfaction. The harder you've had to work in order to win them over, the greater the sense of winning a war. I also felt it was very important that I got across some of my views, that I was able to take a whole new set of comedy targets (i.e. men, Tories, racists and bullies) and extract comedy out of them, to show people that they could laugh at these things as well as mother-in-law jokes and jokes about black or disabled people.

I tried to think about how I could best get into stand-up. There were no comedy courses as such, so I figured the best way was to train as an actress and use that as an in. I applied to drama schools and had about five auditions lined up. The first one was at Mountview Theatre School in Crouch End, and I dutifully learned my prepared pieces and shuffled along there, hoping for the best.

It didn't go well. First of all, a sizeable number of my fellow auditionees struck me as complete drama queens. During the set-piece auditions, one woman did a passage from the play *Saint Joan* and really got stuck in, at one point lying on the floor, foaming at the mouth. I wondered uneasily if she was actually having an epileptic fit and whether I should offer my services, but it was genuinely just VERY BIG acting. She, in fact, was the only one of our group who got a place and, for all I know, she is now Dame Someone-Or-Other.

There was also an improvisation section, and improvisation has been my *bête noire* ever since. The reason for this is that I'm absolutely crap at it. I've always felt that I don't have a fast enough brain to come up with ideas quickly. I think it's always very helpful for an improviser to be a good mimic, and I'm not. The only two impressions I can do are Brian Walden, who was a presenter on political telly shows in the seventies, and a very bad Janet Street-Porter. And, let's face it, that pair aren't particularly going to impress audiences.

We all had a number hung round our necks and were invited to spread ourselves out in the hall. Then we were asked to mime playing a musical instrument. Most people chose something sensible, like a clarinet or a violin, but I decided to give it large and plumped for a church organ. There I was, banging away like a mad woman, when suddenly our two remarkably camp auditioners said, 'Right, that's enough, will you now fold up your instrument and put it on the floor?'

Fuck me, how do you fold up an organ?

Well, I decided I'd better go for it and spent ages running up and down trying to match the corners of the bleeding thing together.

I've always wanted to play the organ, so I was really pleased when the BBC asked me if I'd like to learn an instrument for their *Play It Again* series in 2008, in which so-called celebrities learn to play an instrument. I had an absolutely brilliant six months doing the programme. I was given an organ teacher called Hilary, a very posh bloke who'd worked as head of music at a boys' public school and was also a conductor. The signs weren't good; normally I hate this sort of individual. But he turned out to be an absolute delight and a fantastic teacher. Surprisingly liberal, very funny and kind, he was extremely patient with me as we worked our way through various pieces for different events that were to be filmed. I played a hymn at the church in Benenden, where I went to school, 'Ave Maria' at a wedding in Peckham and a waltz for some dancers at the Tower Ballroom in Blackpool.

I'll give you an idea of what my work days are like occasionally – not quite the twenty minutes' work I'd originally envisaged.

I had to work the day before we filmed at Blackpool, so I drove up there from London the night before. I left London at nine and arrived in Blackpool at two in the morning. I got an alarm call at five thirty and we were filming by six thirty. We did a thirteen-hour day and then, because I had to be back in London the following morning, I drove back that night on three hours' sleep and arrived home at midnight. I'm not touting for sympathy; it's my own fault because I like driving myself. This is because I seem to spend so much of my life talking endlessly to people and I really appreciate having some time on my own in the car, choosing what I listen to and not having to make polite conversation. So it serves me right, obviously.

The denouement of the organ lessons was that I had to play Bach's *Toccata in D Minor* at the Royal Albert Hall during a Christmas concert. I was slotted in as a surprise and I think it is probably the most nervous I have ever been. Mainly because I knew I wasn't allowed to talk to the audience and do jokes. I had all the classic symptoms of extreme anxiety and was slightly worried I might wet myself. I had a dry mouth, my hands were shaking, I felt freezing cold and yet I was sweating, and I was seriously concerned my fingers would turn to jelly and wobble uselessly over the keys.

There were 8,000 people there. Hilary told me not to stop, whatever happened. I sat down at the keys, raised my hands . . . And that's all I remember about it. The whole thing is a complete blur. I didn't stop, I didn't cock up too badly and the whole thing was an absolutely unique experience.

So anyway, after the humiliation of folding the organ was over, we had to stand facing our torturers as they called out our numbers. One by one, we put our hands up and they conferred and put a mark down on their clipboards. When they came to me and I raised my hand in the air, they just pissed themselves laughing, I'm sad to say. Not an actor then.

So I haven't gone for many acting jobs in my career because I was pretty sure I wouldn't get them. I once did a cameo role in Jennifer Saunders' sitcom *Absolutely Fabulous* and got roundly slagged by the critics for my lack of ability.

But my most magical audition, which I simply couldn't turn down, was for a role in Harry Potter, playing a hideous old aunt of Harry who fills up with air and floats up into the sky. When this request came through, my daughter Eliza was only six weeks old, but I just had to go, so I took her with me. It was at a studio just off the M1 and it was a foggy, cold, wintry night. The studio plot was so huge that I was guided through it by a Land Rover. When I arrived, Eliza was asleep and the receptionist sat outside the audition room keeping an eye on her. I went into the room and met the casting director, the Mexican director and someone else, who never really introduced themselves. I had to read two pages of script and was asked to do it about thirteen times. Each time they asked me to do it again, I became slightly more hopeful. They gave absolutely no indication as to whether they thought I was any good and said they would contact me.

They did, the next day, to say I hadn't got it because I was too young, even though I was very good. So that is what I chose to believe, rather than I was crap. Pam Ferris actually got the part and I do not begrudge her it one little bit. She's a brilliant actress whom I've always loved.

Of course, I didn't get into Mountview and I subsequently cancelled the other auditions I had lined up, thinking that I probably couldn't stand the humiliation.

So, in need of some money and some work, I ended up applying to the Maudsley Hospital, where I had trained, for a staff nurse post. This felt like a little defeat in some ways, as I'd had high hopes of people queuing up to give me a job, but in reality I had a degree and a nursing qualification, not an Oxbridge degree and a wealthy mummy and daddy.

I was offered a job at the emergency clinic, which I accepted. The emergency clinic was a wonderful idea and a great department. It operated like a casualty department for people with mental health problems and had no specific catchment area, so anybody that wanted to could walk into the place at any time of the day or night, seven days a week, and request a psychiatric assessment for themselves or a member of their family. It was situated in the outpatients department, for which the nursing team was also responsible, but the clinic had a separate little suite of rooms containing seats and desks in which staff could interview those who had turned up. It operated like casualty too in the sense that people had to wait their turn unless we felt they were too disturbed to sit in a chair. Believe me, there were plenty of those, which meant the poor mild and manageable people had to wait even longer.

This suite of rooms contained the infamous Room One, a larger room with virtually nothing in it, designed to help us staff look after those who were difficult to control and needed more space to pace around in. There was a desk, chair and soft bed beside the wall. Often we had to restrain and sedate people in this room, something none of us liked doing because it made us all feel like Nurse Ratched from *One Flew Over the Cuckoo's Nest*.

As well as running the outpatients department, which meant just checking that the rooms were tidy or occasionally chaperoning doctors who were worried a patient was going to lamp them, we also ran a clinic for those with schizophrenic-type illnesses who were on long-acting medication which required having an injection roughly once a month. These injections were designed to remove the need to take tablets every day. They were known as long-acting phenothiazines, which are basically anti-psychotic drugs to dampen down the symptoms of illnesses like schizophrenia. The monthly injections meant that people who might not be very reliable at taking three tablets three times a day would get the treatment their doctor wanted them to have. Rather than trying to avoid giving huge numbers of injections, I decided this should be an opportunity to get better at it, although I pity the first fifty or so that got my needle in their bums.

What I loved about the emergency clinic was the fact that no two days were the same. Sometimes it was raging, other days very quiet.

Our modus operandi was to take down the details of anyone who pitched up and enter them into a log book, get their notes from our medical records if we already knew them, and assess them. Experienced nurses normally did initial assessments and just collared a doctor to tick a box, in effect, if nothing needed to be done. But in the vast majority of cases, referrals needed to be made or admissions arranged, so the case automatically went on to a doctor.

We also covered the whole of south London for what

are called section 136s. This is a section of the Mental Health Act that the police use in order to remove someone from the streets who is either a risk to themselves or others. In order to stand out in the bustling and action-packed part of London in which we were located, you have to be behaving pretty bloody badly. So when we knew the police were on their way, the atmosphere became more highly charged.

The people we saw could be split into discrete groups: those we'd never met, those we knew vaguely and the regulars. The regulars could be divided up also: patients in the long-term unit, who liked visiting to have a moan, scrounge fags or sit down for a rest in our comfy chairs; and outpatients, who were kind of dependent on us for support and a social life. Quite a few were only too happy to come and tell us when they were pissed, sad, happy or frustrated and they just melded in with the waiting gang of others. Occasionally we had to chuck them out if we were too busy or they were being annoying and intimidating others.

We used to see all sorts of people: old and young, sweet and absolutely horrible, drunk and sober, scary and lovely. It was important to be able to accept that anything was going to happen and any sort of person might come through the door, from a weeping young mother plus baby to a knife-wielding drug dealer; an elderly, confused man to a posh bloke in a suit with depression. Anything went.

Accommodationwise, I started off in the nurses' home and then moved into a fantastic Georgian house in Camberwell, which I shared with the sister of a friend and two male anaesthetists who became my very good friends.

They came in very useful one weekend. I had been to the local dental school to have my wisdom teeth removed, and what this means is letting a student loose on your mouth, which is slightly terrifying. In my case, my dental student was very small and pretty and sweet, but had no strength to speak of and she ended up kneeling on my shoulder in order to get enough purchase to pull out my teeth. Excruciating and farcical all at the same time.

After the deed had been done (she stopped at three because I was very worried I might actually punch her), I lay on the chair, bloodied and defeated, trying to hold it together. She said she'd write me up for some medication. But as I staggered to the pharmacy to collect my mega painkillers, or so I thought, I glanced down at the prescription to see she had written me up for two paracetamol four times a day. I was full of rage but had no more strength left, so I staggered to my car and tried to get home without crashing.

After a few hours at home, the anaesthetic began to wear off and the most appalling pain flooded over me. I have to say that it was even worse than childbirth. I found myself on my hands and knees, crawling round the floor and banging my head on it, in the hope that an alternative source of pain might mask the unbearable drilling pain in my mouth. In desperation, I called one of my flatmates and begged him to bring 'something decent' home for me. Thank the Lord he did, and I spent the weekend in a fog of extraordinarily strong druginess, hallucinating away and thanking my lucky stars I lived with a doctor.

While I was a staff nurse at the emergency clinic, I joined the British Transcultural Society. This was an organisation set up to address the problems faced by ethnic minorities in this country in the arena of psychiatry. For example, four times more Afro-Caribbeans are diagnosed as schizophrenic than the indigenous white population. Unless they really are carrying some stronger gene for schizophrenia, which is completely unlikely, I feel strongly there is some cultural misunderstanding going on. And I saw it in action. One day a very disturbed

Rasta was brought in by the police and we arranged for one of the relatively new junior doctors to see him, a very sweet-natured, white, middle-class man. The Rasta, obviously not happy with his lot, was swearing and abusing all and sundry. As this doctor came in to see him, he was greeted with a torrent of abuse – 'Ras clot, blood clot!' – whereupon the doctor politely enquired whether he was worried he had a blood clot. I had to take him aside and explain. It's a very common Afro-Caribbean term of abuse, which I was told relates to sanitary towels – i.e. blood clot/blood cloth. Perhaps this is true, perhaps it ain't.

There has also been much debate about cannabis psychosis. In other words, can cannabis alone generate a psychotic illness, one which makes you lose touch with reality? Well, on a very simplistic level, I think not. It can certainly exacerbate an existing condition, in my experience, although these days the cannabis on sale seems a great deal stronger than the slightly pathetic makes-you-laugh-makes-you-hungry stuff we used to suck on. I tried something relatively recently called 'Double Zero' and, God, hallucinating and everything. If you believe, as I do, that psychotic illnesses are intimately linked with a chemical imbalance in the brain, the stronger drugs are, the more likely one is to suffer.

From time to time journalists appeared in the emergency clinic, I presume because they thought it would make exciting reading. One journalist from *The Times* stayed for a week and was starting to become a little bit too intrusive. We felt that if, as she wanted, she was to sit in on assessments it was of paramount importance to get the permission of the patient first, so we asked each of them. One day, the police brought in a psychotically depressed woman who had poured petrol on her arms, set fire to them and was a complete mess. She was brought to us first, because they felt she was too disturbed to be treated at casualty and needed sedating. The journalist asked if she could sit in on the assessment. I asked the poor woman in question; I hated doing it. She said no and so we informed the journalist, who seemed very disappointed. While we were trying to get some idea of the poor woman's mental state, the journalist decided to come in anyway and popped her head through the door with a 'can I?' expression on her face which also said, 'I am very important because I am A JOURNALIST.'

I'm afraid I shut her head in the door, and that appeared to discourage her from entering the room any further. Job done.

One group I was very fond of at the emergency clinic was the porters, JJ and Little T. Little T was a youngish ex-army guy, very good looking and a completely lovely bloke who would do anything for you. He was cheeky, liked a laugh and could usually be found at the porters' station, flicking through the paper while keeping an eye out for any signs of trouble. All the patients loved him, and he was so friendly, approachable and down-to-earth with them that he was a huge asset.

JJ was an equally lovely guy. A little bit older and quieter, he was essential to the running of the place. He could be relied upon to be there immediately if trouble started, and even though we did have a huge number of male nurses, I felt much safer if one of the porters was around. Although it wasn't part of their duties, they were always there to back up the female staff and would not hesitate to get involved if it looked like one of us was going to be injured. They saved me a whack on a number of occasions and were invaluable members of our little close-knit family. Also, they used to bring in the most alcohol on Christmas Day. For, yes, I'm afraid quite a few sherries went down throats on Christmas morning, which was normally pretty quiet. And you knew that if anything did happen, it would be dramatic. Early one Christmas morning the police brought in a man who'd jumped out of a first-floor window. When asked why he'd done this, he replied, 'My family were getting on my nerves.' I think we all know how that feels.

After two years as a staff nurse, the senior sister retired, her junior got her job and I was invited to apply for the junior's job.

I'd had a few run-ins with senior staff about my appearance. We didn't wear uniforms because it was felt that distanced us too much from those we were trying to form a relationship with (no, not that sort of relationship). Consequently, everyone's own individual style was on show at work. Most people dressed fairly blandly, but I dressed scruffily, often wearing an ancient, grey, baggy, all-in-one parachuting suit to work.

This had been alluded to on a number of occasions and I had also seen a secret report by senior staff which said I would never be promoted because I dressed too 'Oxfam'.

Despite looking like a bundle of old rags, apparently, I went ahead and applied for the junior sister's job.

Chapter 16

Hitting a Wall

I managed to get the job, despite some reasonably stiff competition, probably because I was a good nurse with a lot of experience and I could manage people. In practical terms, this translated into the fact that nothing appalling in terms of injuries or damage to the place had ever happened on my watch, and I didn't rub people up the wrong way. They all seemed to get on with me. Plus I'd been a staff nurse there for nearly four years, which was unheard of due to the high staff turnover. I had a reasonably good relationship with management, because I kept my mouth shut and did what I was told.

One of the other candidates who applied, also a

staff nurse, didn't get the job and held it against me for quite some time until, thankfully, she left. I did have a bit of trouble adjusting to being in charge. It's always been in my nature to be one of the boys, and it was hard to have authority and be liked at the same time. Despite being a Leo, I am not a natural leader. But I've always thought star signs were bollocks anyway; horoscopes should just be for entertainment. I used to have a soft spot for the ones in the *News of the World*, which was constantly available at the clinic on Sundays, courtesy of one of the porters. Their predictions were always so specific: 'You will meet a man dressed in yellow outside a kebab shop.' It took me about six months to a year to get used to being in charge. There was a senior charge nurse too, so if the going got tough I just passed things up the line to him.

During my time at the Maudsley, the Brixton riots occurred. In fact, there were two lots. The first, in 1981, happened while I was still a student and wasn't actually in south London. The riots that had a major impact on my life were the second lot, in 1985.

Things had been tense between the police and the black community for a while, given the Sus laws, which gave the police carte blanche to stop and search anyone they fancied. As you can imagine, it didn't tend to be old ladies dressed in lilac, dragging shopping trolleys home from Tesco. So when Cherry Groce was accidentally shot and killed by the police in Normandy Road in 1985, the simmer became a boil.

It was the talk of the hospital. Many of our patients lived in or around Brixton and rumours filtered down to us through the more talkative ones. We were told Molotov cocktails were being stockpiled and it was all going to get very nasty.

On the worst few days, we could only sit tight and get on with our caseload. One day, in the midst of all the rioting, the police arrived with someone on a section 136 whom we knew well. He was a long-term attendee who followed a pattern of being sectioned, admitted, stabilised on his drugs and discharged, and then failing to take his tablets or turn up for his injection and being sectioned by the police again. We all marvelled at the fact that in the midst of petrol bombs, fighting, and screeching the police had been able to pick him out of the melee and work out that he needed psychiatric help.

We had an uneasy relationship with the police, who were not famed for their diplomacy and pastoral care in the eighties. I remember once they brought in a woman on a 136 and she arrived in the department completely naked, handcuffed to a young policeman. I was appalled at the lack of dignity accorded her and wondered if it would have made any difference if she had been white. Someone ran to get a blanket to cover her while the young policeman got on the phone to his sergeant and very loudly proclaimed to most of the outpatients department: 'We're at the Maudsley, sarge, trying to find out whevver she's a nutter or not.'

On another occasion, a police van screeched to a halt outside the department on a Sunday morning and out jumped six policemen carrying a man who some while earlier had been arrested in a graveyard. Just before they grabbed him, he caught a pigeon, bit the head off and stuffed it down his throat. By the time the police brought him in, he was a purple colour and we immediately dispatched him to Room One, hung him upside down, banged him on the back and out flew the remains of the pigeon. I asked the policeman in charge why they had not attempted to remove the pigeon to stop the man choking. His answer? 'Well, we did, love, but he made so much fucking noise, we shoved it back in again.'

That evening, as I was heading home from work, I braked at the lights on Denmark Hill and sailing past me went a stark-naked woman on a bicycle, with her hair flying out behind her like some modern-day Lady Godiva. She looked magnificent but, of course, rather incongruous in the south London traffic. I wondered how far she'd get before the police spotted her and if they'd take her to the clinic. I came in the next morning to discover she had indeed been brought in, but had managed to get as far as the Elephant and Castle, a good four miles.

On another occasion a patient I knew, who was as gentle as anything when he was well, but quite dangerous when ill, was brought in on a 136. I sat him down in a chair and asked how he was. He opened his mouth to speak and most of his teeth tumbled out. By the time I had a moment to ask the police who had delivered him and what had gone on in the van, they had disappeared, having signed him over to us. I decided to make a formal complaint – the only one I made throughout my entire nursing career. So I wrote a letter to the relevant department, and waited ... and waited ... and waited. Several months later, I received a summons to see a very senior police officer and was interviewed in his office. I told my story very matter-of-factly with the minimum of emotion. At one point during my story the officer intervened and asked whether it was possible that any members of staff at the emergency clinic had knocked the man's teeth out. I was pretty upset by this, considering that when the incident had occurred there had been just myself and another female nurse on duty.

The outcome was somewhat unsatisfactory: not much happened and the police were angry about the complaint. On a number of occasions, when we called for help because of a violent incident, they seemed to be dragging their feet. I'd like to think things have changed, and friends still in the biz say it's better. I've met so many really good policemen in my time, so I have never felt the poison is all-pervasive, but it certainly depressed me as a nurse.

My appearance came up for some more criticism once I was promoted, as I think it was felt that I should slip into a twin-set and pearls.

I suppose I am just a natural scruffbag. I don't have the ability to look smart and stay looking smart. Even if I make a supreme effort to get dressed up, something always happens to spoil it, like me spilling food down myself, or someone's child wiping a bogey on me. I think some women have the ability to maintain their sartorial dignity whatever the challenges, and I'd love to be able to do that. I have always been very last minute, and so some days, if I got up late for work, which I frequently did because an extra ten minutes in bed was more important to me than being smartly turned out, I found myself with about thirty seconds to get ready. I'd pull stuff out of the washing basket, compare it to see which item looked the least dirty, maybe scrub at unsightly stains with a dishcloth. I am the antithesis of Anthea Turner. My room – wherever it was, be it in student halls or a shared house – was always a complete tip, with overflowing ashtrays, records and CDs scattered everywhere, old cups with mould in them, unmade bed, drawers full of unwearable clothes and a general air of chaos.

Also, I absolutely bloody hate shopping, always have. I cannot understand the whole concept of retail therapy. To me, shopping involves slogging round hot, sweaty buildings full of snooty assistants who look at chubby losers like me as if we are the scum of the earth, or being battered about in tiny changing rooms with girls who weigh three stone and always have on the most attractive underwear you can imagine, while I, with my too-old Marks and Sparks pants and bra, cower in the corner waiting for an opportunity to try something on when there is no one in there, which, in a busy department store, is never.

That's why being asked to do Trinny and Susannah

in 2003 made me roar with laughter. I suppose I agreed to do it because I was fascinated to see just what kind of hideous garment they would come up with for me. Plus I wanted to give as good as I got on behalf of all those women who do not take great joy in their appearance and who just want to get through the day without their clothes either falling off or being covered in food.

The resulting outfit was fucking hilarious: a creepy, brown two-piece suit with a fairly tight top with a plunging neckline (which I hate, I've never liked cleavage, not sure why, just think it looks horrible) and a long, flared skirt and ridiculously high-heeled, uncomfortable shoes. The practical result of very high-heeled shoes is that you can't bloody run in them, and I think there are plenty of times in a woman's life when she needs to run.

So anyway, when I was a nurse my clothes were either purchased in charity shops, given to me by others or grabbed in a head-down run through a clothes shop, a bit like *Supermarket Sweep*. I gave up trying things on because it was such a bloody nightmare, so half the stuff I bought didn't fit properly and looked shit, and that kind of became my style. And that just was not acceptable for a senior nurse, apparently.

I made every effort not to get sucked into the New

Romantic fashion phase, because, although I am a scruffbag, I am a scruffbag who knows what I like and New Romantics were the most ridiculous set of individuals I had set eyes on since Glitter Rock in the seventies. Especially the blokes. They all looked like disturbed, effeminate pirates to me. I stuck steadfastly to my uniform of baggy T-shirts and jumpers, workmen's dungarees, monkey boots and a donkey jacket. I was a big fan of Michael Foot, who was the Labour Party leader for a while. There was an enormous fuss in the press about him wearing a so-called 'donkey jacket' to a First World War commemorative event at the Cenotaph because royalty were there. Jesus Christ, I remember thinking to myself, haven't they got anything better to talk about? Michael Foot was someone, in my opinion, who should probably not have been in politics – he was far too nice. A sensitive, educated man who looked slightly eccentric, he allowed the press to rip him to shreds and ruin any credibility he had.

My social life outside work was a mixture of things. I was part of a big, friendly, amorphous group that would expand and contract depending on who was around. The people on the degree course tended to stick together, and our social lives were mainly based in the pub and at parties, with the occasional gig or trip to the theatre thrown in when we could be bothered.

I sometimes went to the theatre with my very good friend Helen, who was on the same course as me but the year below. Once she decided to go for a rather dramatic haircut, as she was going to the wedding of one of her boyfriend's relatives. In fact, she had the sides of her head shaved and looked like a Mohican princess. The night before she was due to go to the wedding, she and I went to see *Piaf* starring Jane Lapotaire, a famous West End and TV actress at the time. We didn't really enjoy the production and left at the interval, both of us in quite bad moods because of the amount of money we had wasted. A theatre employee asked as we passed, 'And where are you two *ladies* going?' in as sarcastic a voice as he could manage, to which Helen replied, 'We're leaving 'cause the play's shit.' Quite pleased with her riposte, we carried on walking, and his voice came floating through the air behind us: 'So's your hair, dear.' Touché.

Every year for a few years we would go away at New Year and stay up in the Lake District for a week. I tacked on to a group of Helen's friends, who did this as a regular thing. We would hire two big cottages and there would be about fifteen of us, a mixture of men, women, singles and couples. It worked pretty well. We would go for long walks during the day, up peaks like Helvellyn, and then get rat-arsed in the pub every night.

One year it was particularly cold and there was a lot of snow on the ground, so we decided to go sledging. We managed to get hold of a couple of trays, bought a couple of cheap sledges and set off up the side of a very steep hill. I ended up on a sledge with the girlfriend of a doctor who I was eventually to share a house with a year or so later. We were on one of the proper sledges and set off, her on the front, me on the back, whooping and screeching as we whizzed through the sharp, frosty air. I'm not sure at what point it dawned on us that we were heading for a massive dry-stone wall at about thirty miles an hour, but we didn't have very long to plan our strategy of evasion.

We just threw ourselves off in an effort not to get knocked unconscious or worse. In the process, my fingers were bent backwards onto my hand as they got caught under the sledge and I felt a sharp pain and a cracking noise. We picked ourselves up from the ground. Of course everyone was pissing themselves laughing.

Over the next couple of hours my hand began to swell alarmingly, so I was taken off to the local casualty, which was the tiniest, sweetest little place you have ever seen, and seemed to be staffed by one nurse and one doctor. The doctor, I remember, looked about twelve and was wearing the most hideous knitted tank top I had ever seen (one of *those* Christmas presents). His treatment for me, after having ascertained that I had broken my knuckle, was to bandage my hand very tightly, with my fingers bent round a cotton reel. I wondered if he was a bit bonkers. Back in London, I was referred for physiotherapy at my local hospital, where they laughed their heads off at the cotton reel and made me plunge my hand into a bowl of ice for ten minutes every day for two weeks. It was SO PAINFUL. And my hand never got any better.

Anyway, back to nursing. I'd toned down my appearance as much as I possibly could, but was not prepared to go to work looking like a Sunday school teacher. Consequently, I received a letter from the chief nursing officer saying there were 'some concerns' about my dress. By this point, I was really fed up. I felt I'd worked my bollocks off in the job and we had a department that ran as smoothly as it could given the challenges we faced, and all they could do was whine on about how I looked! In a temper, possibly hormonally motivated,

I sat down and wrote a letter of resignation. I had no idea what I'd do if they accepted it; it was really a challenge to the hospital, to see whether they would allow someone to leave because of something relatively trivial. Thank God, as soon as the chief nursing officer received my letter, she called me to her office and backed down. One of the few battles I have won.

Not long after this the senior charge nurse left and I was promoted to his level. By then I'd been there four years or so. The average turnover was six months for qualified staff, as the department was considered so stressful and not everyone was suited to the emotionally charged atmosphere of a place like that. One thing that the NHS doesn't seem to be able to do is sack bad staff. The tendency is to move them round the hospital till they've been on every ward and then start again at the beginning.

I was asked by one of the nurse managers to take a staff nurse who was struggling on another ward. I pointed out that we were not the best place for someone who had a record of being rather awkward and sometimes inappropriately censorious with patients. He would not have it, though, so we agreed to a month trial.

Unfortunately, within a week, an incident occurred which secured her propulsion back whence she came.

Someone we knew very well came in in a highly agitated state, demanding to be seen. I would have taken him off to a quiet room and got a doctor to see him immediately. Our new nurse didn't really know him and didn't ask anyone about him. Instead, she turned to him with a headmistressy expression on her face and said, 'Sit down and wait your turn.' I'm afraid she got her face punched, resulting in a broken nose, and although all our clients had to be held responsible for their acts of violence, it could have been so easily avoided.

But most of the nurses at the emergency clinic were brilliant, from the West Indian nursing assistant who could handle anyone in any given situation and fed us regularly with enormous amounts of homemade curry to a state-enrolled nurse called Kristina, who is still a really close friend of mine. She was the one person I always wanted with me when the going got really rough. This was because Kristina was so approachable, straightforward and instinctively knew what to do in those situations. Her working-class roots shone through, and when you are facing some hulking, great, angry Camberwell brute, the last thing you want is a Sophie from Hampstead with a Cambridge degree in social relations. Kristina formed great relationships with all the regulars and they loved her to bits. She was the biggest asset we had. Of course, she had a bad side, we all do. She could be argumentative, stubborn and annoying at times. But these traits paled into insignificance when she got stuck into a situation and saw it through to the bitter end.

Sadly, Kristina had only been at the clinic a month or so when she became ill, with some numbness and difficulty walking. She was immediately admitted to the general hospital over the road from us and a few days later was diagnosed as having MS. What a nightmare: new job in London, didn't know anyone and the prospect of a deteriorating body to look forward to.

Myself and the junior charge nurse, a fantastic, feisty woman called Frankie, between us managed to visit her almost every day for three months and things gradually improved. Kristina is still going strong today and I suspect, although I have no medical evidence to back this up, that she fought the illness in the right way, by simply refusing to acknowledge it or give in to it.

I still see Frankie to this day as well. She has a brilliant, sardonic sense of humour of the most biting kind and this would be turned on everyone. She was gorgeous-looking too, blonde, blue-eyed and buxom. Later on she lost quite a bit of weight and I always berated her about it, but she'd just tell me to fuck off and mind my own business. She is absolutely loaded with common sense too. This is a much-maligned characteristic in my eyes. I saw many nurses over the years make ridiculous decisions because they fell back on the textbooks rather than use some gumption.

There were times when things did go horribly wrong. One day the police brought in an absolutely huge Irishman from a building site. He was hypomanic – talking nineteen to the dozen and threatening people – and generally very scary. He was about 6ft 6ins and weighed approximately twenty-five stone. On very rare occasions, if we felt we didn't have the manpower, we would ask the police to stay, so we all tramped into Room One with this man. There were probably about six policemen and six nurses, and we tried to contain him while we awaited our poor senior registrar, who had to assess him. The senior reg, a lovely doctor who was mild-mannered, very funny and very sweet-tempered, arrived and began to question our patient. Within seconds, it all went wrong. Our patient managed to land a huge punch under the chin of the doctor, lifting him up in the air and knocking him unconscious. Pandemonium ensued. The police and we nurses immediately jumped on the patient while someone dragged the doctor out of the room. He came round pretty quickly and another doctor was immediately called to sort things out. She prescribed intravenous Valium, which is a last resort, to enable someone to be sedated really quickly. I've only seen it used this one time. We all held the guy down, the needle went into his arm and he was sparko immediately.

Now, I'm sure this is not an easy image for people to assimilate. It sounds awful and, believe you me, it looks awful. I am not naive enough to think that cruelty of some sort doesn't go on in psychiatric institutions, but I can honestly say, with my hand on my heart, that I never once witnessed any behaviour of that sort by a nurse, not even the use of slightly too much force.

The difficulty with big institutions like psychiatric hospitals is that they are bureaucratic and a very narrow set of rules has to cover all situations, which makes creative imagination redundant. One size has to fit all. The staff, as well as the patients, can quickly become institution-alised, and it is easy for hospitals to become closed, inward-looking institutions in which the staff behave weirdly. I fought against this sort of thing all my working life. I wanted staff to look outwards and take into account what was happening in society.

Given MIND's remit, there were occasionally times when we would clash with them. One day, someone we knew very well arrived at the department in a highly psychotic state. We knew that the very slightest thing would result in violence on his part, so we were tiptoeing round him as he ranged through the outpatients department, muttering threats and looking very frightening. Initially we didn't have enough staff to restrain him and he refused to come into a room, so we just had to keep an eye on him and protect the other patients until we could get enough staff together to handle the situation. In the meantime, someone had arrived from MIND for a meeting and was sitting in the middle of it all, watching and appearing to take notes.

MIND is an organisation set up to protect the rights of the users of psychiatric services, and rightly so. But occasionally our impression of them was that they were actively seeking to witness abusive behaviour. In a situation in which you have to restrain someone, it is sometimes going to look like some abuse is going on, so we were a bit wary.

Eventually we had enough staff to be safe and we tried to persuade the man to come into a room. He absolutely refused, as he must have realised somewhere in his disturbed mind that we were going to section and admit him. He positioned himself at the far end of the department, a long way from our rooms, so we were forced to approach and restrain him in the middle of a busy outpatients department. And it was a real fight. He was as strong as anything and a huge scuffle ensued, with arms flailing and people being hit. Eventually we restrained him and injected him on the spot with a tranquilliser, right next to the guy from MIND, who continued to take notes. We were never approached by MIND about this incident, so I presume we did the right thing.

There were several families in the Camberwell area who were a real handful. One big Irish family, who all had alcohol and personality problems, would very occasionally arrive in one big, drunken, threatening mass. One day they all pitched up and when they were asked to come back when they were sober they set about smashing up the place. There were so many of them we felt it was beyond the call of duty to tackle them. Thankfully, there was no one else there, as it was a weekend. So we locked ourselves in a room, called the police and listened to the music of chairs smashing and tables flying.

In 1987, a friend of my mother's who ran a nursing home needed an RMN (a qualified psychiatric nurse) to cover the place while she went away for a few days and asked me if I would do it. Despite the fact that I was rather scared of the responsibility, I agreed. I'm a bit crap at saying no.

The place had a lot of elderly residents, so in some ways it was like an old people's home, but there were also a few younger people there with physical disabilities and/or learning disabilities. My favourite was a young man who had been in a motorbike accident and had brain damage. He had a customised wheelchair which he operated with incredible agility. He wasn't an easy character to manage because he had no ability to control his temper at all and he would fly into huge rages during which he would lash out at staff. Pragmatically speaking, though, all one had to do was get out of the range of his wheelchair and the problem was sorted. I became very fond of him over a few days and could easily understand the anger inside him. He had gone from a promising life of endless possibility to being shoved in a wheelchair, leading a miserable existence in the company of mainly elderly people. But he did his best to maintain his independence.

One night, as he did most nights, he went off in his wheelchair to get pissed at a local pub. At about midnight, the doorbell rang and I opened the door to find him in his wheelchair, flanked by two policemen.

They had caught him speeding, doing forty miles an hour in a thirty-mile-an-hour zone. He managed this because the home stood on a very long hill that ran all the way down to the sea and if he got himself to the top, he could get up a tremendous speed. I admired his spirit so much and when the police had gone, he and I had a really good laugh about it. They didn't press charges.

While I was at the home, the 1987 election occurred and Margaret Thatcher got re-elected. God, what a depressing day that was and what an irony that Britain's first female prime minister had to be Margaret Thatcher. She was the woman who asked, 'What has feminism ever done for me?' Well, dear, if you need to ask that question then you're obviously not very bright.

Chapter 17

'Please Welcome
The Sea Monster'

I suppose eventually I realised I was edging towards thirty without having had a crack at comedy, and a sort of desperation started to seep in. Besides, the more senior I became at work, the more I didn't want to go down the road of becoming a manager, stuck in some office ordering toilet rolls and having hair like my grandma's. I know that's simplistic, but it seemed that the more qualified you got, the less you used what you'd learned.

Round about this time, a friend of mine, to whom I constantly moaned about wanting to do comedy, told me to get off my arse and do something about it, using words to the effect that we don't get a second go at life. I suppose the combination of being twenty-nine and him telling me to pull my finger out did spur me into some sort of action. So-called 'alternative comedy' was in its infancy, with the birth of the Comedy Store and numerous little clubs springing up all over London.

The Comedy Store was the glamour end of the comedy market because of its Americanness. It had a very in-your-face logo of a red laughing mouth and everything about it screamed American import. Although in the eighties it was considered part of the alternative comedy scene, in some ways it was quite mainstream. It didn't really epitomise so-called 'alternative' values. It was quite expensive to get into, it was situated in the heart of the West End, it employed bouncers and it tended to attract an out-of-town crowd from the suburbs of London rather than a regular, faithful audience. There were two stand-up shows on a Friday and Saturday, an early one at 7.30 and a late one starting at midnight.

The other comedy clubs (apart from Jongleurs, which was similar to the Store in some ways but catered to a more upmarket crowd of City types and people from Clapham) were a much more eclectic mix, ranging from a vegetarian cafe on the Archway Road, to a room above a pub just off Carnaby Street, to a Labour club in Finsbury Park called the Red Rose. They all had their own particular character and audience – some friendly, some snooty, some aggressive, some apathetic, some wild and some miserable.

I didn't really go to comedy shows at that time. I didn't want to watch it, I wanted to do it. I found it frustrating to watch it when I wanted to have a crack myself and I didn't want other people's influences to seep into what I was doing. So I avoided comedy, weirdly. I don't have the male-comic mentality, which seems to be quite common and involves watching endlessly everything your favourite comics have ever done on DVD.

Work was changing. The NHS was being transformed by Thatcher and I wasn't sure I could tolerate it. Gradually, sections of the NHS were being shaved off and farmed out to private companies.

As luck would have it, another friend, coincidentally the girlfriend of Mr Get-Your-Finger-Out, was organising a benefit for Greenpeace or some such charity and she suggested that this was finally my opportunity to try out a bit of stand-up without having to make any effort whatsoever. It was on a plate for me.

So I decided to go for it. The benefit was being held in a nightclub in Soho. (My experience since has taught me that nightclubs are not really the best places to do comedy benefits in. It's not that there's something intrinsically bad about them, but comedy just doesn't seem to work so well as it does in a 'proper' comedy club.)

I was blissfully ignorant of the ins and outs of live stand-up comedy, and so I set about preparing my five minutes. I'd been told that there were three booked comics to perform first and I would be on at the end. This just would not happen in most comedy clubs. New performers doing what is known as an 'open spot' or 'guest spot' tend to be put in the middle of the bill, to shield them from an unwarmed-up audience or a completely pissed-up one.

I didn't know what sort of stuff to do for my little five-minute act, but I had two weeks or so to come up with it and thought I should stick to what I knew. I prepared five minutes on Sigmund Freud and psycho-analysis because I remembered it from college, but I suppose it was slightly above the grasp of most ordinary people and bloody dull to boot. The problem with stand-up material is that you cannot try it out on anyone other than a comedy audience. And however much your friends tell you that you are hysterically funny, it is impossible for them to judge your one-liners in an unbiased way.

The night finally arrived and, even though I didn't think it was possible, my anxiety increased somewhat, rising to an almost unmanageable level by the time I arrived at the club to do my bit.

The Soho nightclub was a slightly dingy place. It had a surface glamour, but beneath that there was a faint smell of stale beer and fags. This is what nightclubs are all about. They're usually dark so you can't see the peeling paint and slight scruffiness. I suspect people are encouraged to get drunk so that it doesn't occur to them, in a massively depressing way, that they are in a painted box with surly staff, trying to have a good time but failing miserably on that count more often than not.

The shape of the venue was all wrong. A makeshift stage had been knocked up and the lighting was the normal club lighting so the act on stage didn't particularly stand out. There were around 200 people there.

It began to dawn on me fairly early on in the evening that the audience was not a particularly good one. They were a bit listless, hot and chatty, and this wasn't helped by the fact that the sightlines weren't great and the acoustics were crap as well.

As the evening went on and the pure, unadulterated fear in the pit of my stomach began to get out of control, I medicated myself with lager and the edges of the world became more blurred as the evening went on. The show began to run really late. Several times I considered just forgetting the whole thing and walking out of the place, never to return to the world of stand-up, but something made me stay there. Eventually, it was time to go on. It was midnight, everyone was pissed, I was pissed, and through the haze I heard the compere announce my name. At that point, I thought it would probably be a success if I could actually stand up for five minutes and not piss myself.

Almost the second I set foot on stage someone at the back started to heckle me with the words, 'Fuck off, you fat cow!' As it was my first time, I'd assumed that at a benefit people would be nice and I had not considered having to deal with hecklers, so I had no idea what to do. I started to struggle very badly through my prepared material. Quite a lot of people obviously didn't know what the fuck I was talking about, and my heckler didn't just stop at one 'Fuck off, you fat cow!' He repeated it over and over and over again, until after a couple of minutes I couldn't take any more and I did fuck off.

I can't really remember what I felt afterwards, insulated as I was by vast amounts of alcohol. People were randomly patting me in a three-quarters sympathetic, one-quarter admiring way, probably not because of my material, but rather for just getting through it without crying. Many people have asked me since how on earth I got over such a humiliation and carried on. Well, the truth of it is that I was so off my face, I don't particularly remember it being that humiliating. Afterwards, I tried not to think too much about it or my entrails would twitch and I would blush, sitting there on my own in my bedroom.

I subsequently found out that my tormentor, the very clever heckler, was in fact another comedian on the circuit. He came as a pair with another comic and they had a reputation for being somewhat anarchic and encouraging events that they were at to descend into chaos. But to shout 'Fuck off' at a fat woman isn't that anarchic in my book. Men have been doing it for years. It's extraordinarily boring if you're on the receiving end of it, because you've heard it so often, and yet they think they are the first one ever to say it to you.

This first comedy performance took place in the summer of 1986 and I felt like I needed a little breathing space before I had another crack at it, so I left it until the autumn before I stepped on stage again. During this time I met Malcolm, a performer and club promoter, with whom I had a relationship for a while. He was known as a 'character', given as he was to massively unpredictable bouts of out-of-control behaviour, but he was enormously entertaining and funny. At the time, he was part of a comedy group whose most famous number was 'The Balloon Dance', a charming line dance by a trio of naked men with balloons covering their genitals. As the dance progressed, they would snatch at each other's balloons, with hilarious results.

On my first date with Malcolm he was arrested for jumping a red light at the Elephant and Castle and was stuck in the cells for a few hours. That set the pattern for a chaotic friendship that lasted a long time. Malcolm drowned in the Thames some years ago and every time I drive over it, which is a lot, I think of him.

I decided that, at the very least, I should have a bash at a proper comedy club with a slightly different act which was perhaps a bit simpler and a lot funnier. So I managed to get a five-minute spot at a comedy club in New Cross in south London. It was a bit of a relief to get in there and find that the audience were expecting comedy, they weren't drunk and they were sat in rows looking reasonably un-homicidal.

I'd completely changed my five minutes, throwing out all the Freud rubbish and preparing a selection of one-liners. I called myself the Sea Monster, because I didn't want people at work to find out what I was up to. The reason I chose the Sea Monster was because it was utterly ridiculous and a friend of Malcolm's used to call me that, in a fond rather than abusive way (I hope). I had managed to work a joke round it too, to do with a boyfriend who wanted us to split up so I said that I had made certain promises to him, the final one being that I would become a stand-up comic with a ridiculous name.

I wanted an opening line that had a bit of drama to it, so I worked out something very unpalatable. I wore a big, white, baggy T-shirt and just before the compere announced me, I put a blood capsule from a joke shop in my mouth. As I came onto the stage and stood in front of the mic, I started coughing violently and what looked like blood shot out of my mouth and all over my T-shirt, at which point I said, 'Oh dear, must give up smoking.'

Well, I thought this was hugely amusing and so did roughly half the audience. The other half just thought it was tasteless, which it was. However, it set me off on the right track and, for only a second gig, it went shockingly, surprisingly well. At the end of the show, a woman who was putting a Christmas variety show together at the Gate Theatre in Notting Hill came up and took my number and asked me if I would do three nights there. I was gobsmacked. My first booking. Couldn't quite believe it.

My strategy vis-à-vis how I would progress was to do the easy clubs first. I figured there was no point launching into the difficult clubs and being demoralised by being murdered on stage. I had started to meet a few comics and chat to them, and I learned that the clubs considered to be really hard at the time were the Comedy Store in Leicester Square, Jongleurs and the Tunnel Club, which sat very unattractively at the entrance to the Blackwall Tunnel, an area reminiscent of some futuristic, industrial wasteland.

The Comedy Store wasn't easy, mainly because it had a late show that started at midnight. It tended to attract groups of women and men, some on stag and hen nights, and it was especially appalling on a Friday night, as the late-night audience would have been drinking solidly since they got out of work.

Jongleurs in Battersea (there are now loads of them,

but there was only one in the eighties) had a reputation for attracting young, urban professionals (or yuppies) and that was enough of a nightmare in itself. Wealthy, cocky and extremely irritating would be my in-depth analysis of them. So not my favourite place.

The Tunnel Club had an identity of its own and was blessed with an unruly, pissed and rather clever audience – as one, they would randomly pick on an act and do their best to destroy them, whether they were any good or not. I once saw them lay into Harry Enfield, who was doing brilliantly, and then give someone who told a ten-minute joke in Serbo-Croat a standing ovation.

Having done a few try-out spots between my second gig and Christmas, I finally arrived at my first booking at the Gate Theatre. By this time I had had an opportunity to hone my new material, chuck out the dead wood and write a bit more, but I was still slightly anxious as I drove up to Notting Hill, because here was another milestone – a gig I had ACTUALLY BEEN ASKED TO DO.

Each time something new happened in my comedy career, it was an opportunity to learn something, and I learned a very important lesson at the Gate Theatre.

I was waiting backstage to go on and heard the compere announce my name and the audience start clapping. In a panic, I realised I didn't know how to get on to the stage, rule number one, surely, in the stand-up comic's manual. Blindly, I ran around in the dark. Edging closer to where the applause was starting to die out to a smatter and seeing no slit in the dark curtain, I dived underneath and came out the other side . . . on stage. The audience, seeing me crawling out from under the curtain at the back of the stage, pissed themselves laughing, so I had to pretend I'd done it deliberately. I sauntered as nonchalantly as I could up to the mic . . . and then couldn't get the bloody thing off the stand. I got so desperate that eventually I forced it out and broke the clip – another big laugh.

I decided I could not go on having the technical ability of a three year old and should take on board some stage nous double-quick.

Chapter 18

Sitting in Cars with Funny People

As my comedy career started to stagger forwards bit by bit, I was still trying to hold on to my job at the emergency clinic. In lots of ways, the nursing job on its own was stressful enough and I found it hard to fit the gigs in around the proper job. Once I had been going for about six to eight months, doing small gigs round London, I started to get work outside the metropolis and that involved seriously long drives, say to Nottingham, to do a show and then back the same night and maybe an early shift at 7.15 the next morning. I was beginning to get bloody exhausted.

By this time, I had bought a flat with a friend, Sue, and so more than ever needed some sort of steady income to pay the mortgage, and what I got from my comedy wasn't quite enough.

I also had to fit a rather hectic social life into all this, as there were numerous parties to go to and a life to lead. Occasionally I would do extremely stupid things. I could make the excuse that this was down to tiredness, but mainly it was down to me being an arse.

One night, very drunk, I drove back from a party with a few people in my little car. When we got to the flat where I lived with Sue, a thirties' block, in order to entertain the people in the car, I drove on to the middle of the ornamental garden and raced round and round it, all of us hysterical with laughter. What I had not realised was that a police van had followed us up the hill, seen me go through some red lights and followed the car to the flats. I was blissfully unaware of this and the copper just sat in his van and watched as I drove everyone round and round the garden. When I eventually parked up and we began to get out of the car, the policeman strolled over and asked whether I'd been drinking. The problem was that I'd got to that bolshy stage of couldn't-give-a-toss, so rather than trying to play it down and get myself out of trouble, I upped it. 'I should say so,' I replied cheerily.

He breathalysed me and said that I was way over the limit and would have to go to the station, at which point I remarked, 'It's a fair cop.' (Yes, very unoriginal, I know.)

At this point, thankfully, Sue intervened and explained that I was the senior sister at the emergency clinic, I'd had a very stressful week, I'd never done anything like this before and I was very sorry and wouldn't do it again. Amazingly, the policeman turned to me and said, 'All right, get inside before I change my mind.' I did.

The following week, during a particularly busy day at work, a policeman wandered up to the front desk and said 'Remember me?' I didn't, but he was in fact the copper who had nearly arrested me, just checking that I was who Sue had said I was. I was a big supporter of the police that week.

I was being given more responsibility at work and a few times a month I was actually allowed to be in charge of the entire hospital, which rather surprised me. I must admit I tend to deal with pressure like that by ignoring it. So I never felt too anxious, although one worry was that someone would die in the hospital while I was in charge, because although I knew what I should do in theory, I had never actually put it into practice and hoped I would never have to. I didn't.

One day, the night charge nurse turned up quite obviously pissed. He smelled of drink, his speech was slurred and I immediately phoned my senior, who agreed to come in. We both assessed him as pretty drunk and he was asked to go home while cover was found.

What upset me about this was that when some disciplinary action was taken, he asked the union rep to be present with him and, even though we knew each other well, the union rep seemed to be implying that I was racist, because the guy was black and I didn't understand the cultural differences between white and black drinking. What a load of bollocks! I am a big supporter of unions, but I think occasionally they do themselves a disservice. This kind of thing dilutes the seriousness of genuine cases of racism, of which there are quite a few in large institutions.

These sorts of situations made me feel even more demoralised at work. It was a very unwieldy place that was no doubt difficult to run, and it was starting to get to me a bit. I was gradually getting more stand-up bookings and was beginning to feel that if I stayed much longer I would have no choice but to become as institutionalised as the long-serving members of staff. I decided that soon there would have to be a cut-off point when I would risk letting go of my massive nursing salary and take a chance on comedy.

Much of my early comedy act revolved around my weight. This was for a few reasons. First of all, I knew it was the first thing people would notice about me when I stepped on stage. Secondly, it was something that some individuals in the street thought was obligatory to comment on, and I wanted some right of reply. Thirdly, I thought that if I tackled the issue in a self-deprecating way, it would fend off the worst of the hecklers in the audience. Also, if I got that out of the way and had the audience on my side, then I'd be free to tackle other topics that were perhaps more difficult for some of them to swallow, like having a go at men, for example.

So some of my early jokes about my weight were:

'I was the child who was asked to play Bethlehem in the school nativity play.'

'I went to a health farm, ended up eating my bedroom.'

'I went on the pill when I was sixteen and put on four stone, so that proved to be a very effective contraceptive.'

I tended to write what I would call very spare

material. There was no padding at all, and because I was nervous, not a natural performer and probably not a good public speaker either, I'd keep my lines short and simple rather than digress. At the beginning of my career, I learned everything word for word and repeated it parrot-fashion, and I found it excruciating if I was forced to stray from my prepared material. Everyone thought I had a weird style because I delivered stuff in a world-weary monotone. This wasn't deliberate; it just happened because I had no idea how to deliver jokes and my nervousness made my voice sound like that.

One thing I found absolutely amazing was the first time I saw my name printed in the listings mags – *Time Out* and *City Limits*. I sat and stared at it for ages and couldn't quite believe it was there. I felt a mixture of pride and wonder and was gobsmacked that I was on the road to achieving something.

I particularly loved *City Limits*, the listings magazine that is no longer with us. It was well known for misprints, and sometimes they inadvertently hit the nail on the head. I remember their listing for an all-female stand-up show. The headline at the top announced an 'ALL WOMEN SHOW!' And underneath the names were listed:

Jenny Lecoat
Donna McPhail
Hattie Hayridge
Jo Brand
Bernard Gilhooly

'Bernard' Gilhooly was, of course, Brenda Gilhooly, an utterly charming, friendly and delightful stand-up whose path I crossed many times on the circuit and who became a good friend. She did straight stand-up for a while and then developed a very funny character called Gayle Tuesday, an ex-Page Three model. She now works with Harry Hill and, as we both have families, our busy lives dictate that we don't see each other as much as we'd like.

There was also another brilliant misprint about Brenda which was quite prescient considering the character she ended up doing. *City Limits* used to abbreviate certain words to give you a flavour of what the comic was like, and one of their favourites was 'sexpol' – i.e. sexual politics. Once while trawling the listings, I saw 'Brenda Gilhooly (sexpot)'. Not quite the effect *City Limits* intended.

The comedy I performed early on was deliberately designed to shock. This is because I've never been a fan of euphemism. I've always liked to tell it like it is. I find that genteel, slightly middle-class attitude that calls, for example, dying 'passing away' or having a mental illness 'a breakdown' very irritating. And I think there are far too many euphemisms in the whole area of bodily functions. It is the British disease and probably the reason we all have such a weird attitude towards sex and toilet subjects. If you look at traditional comics, their jokes were peppered with euphemisms, but the meaning underneath was very clear to everyone, so why not just say it? I think women are made to feel ashamed of having periods, for example. In some cultures, women are sent away from society for the duration of their periods, for God's sake. So I wanted to say it like it was.

Hence: 'Lots of people use euphemisms for periods, because it's embarrassing, like "I've got the painters and decorators in" or "Arsenal are playing at home". I prefer "I've got a vast amount of blood squirting out of my cunt, Vicar".' I used to finish my set with that, and I can see why some people fainted (only kidding).

In my first year of stand-up, I did quite a few 'open spots' in all the clubs around London. On the whole they went well and I can't remember any huge disasters. I worked with a wide range of different comics who were around at the time: Julian Clary – no different from how he is today; Eddie Izzard – absolutely terrible when he started, just not funny. In fact, poor old Eddie, it became a standing joke: 'Eddie's died again.'

And then one night, at the Red Rose Labour Club, we were steeling ourselves for Eddie to have another nightmare, feeling sorry for him because we all liked him, and, out of the blue, he absolutely stormed it. The crowd went mental, gave him an encore and he never looked back. It was interesting because he hadn't changed his material much, but he'd somehow shifted the emphasis of his delivery slightly and added a bit more of a surreal touch to it. Such is the very thin line between funny and dreadful.

Frank Skinner was the same. I first saw him at a club in Birmingham soon after he'd started and he really struggled. I had him down as a no-hoper and yet when I saw him a few months later, he had found a way of delivering that worked and the audience loved him.

Other comics floating around at that time were Mark Thomas, Rob Newman, Dave Baddiel, Hattie Hayridge, Harry Hill, Al Murray, Alan Davies and Mark Lamarr, all of whom were really good stand-ups. My favourites at the time were Nick Hancock and Lee Cornes. We all used to love Hancock's set, to the point that we knew much of it by heart and would mouth it along with him at the Comedy Store.

Lee Cornes, who never really went mega (I don't know why because he was brilliant), ended up playing a science teacher in *Grange Hill*. His act was a lesson in taking the piss. He was once compering at the Comedy Store and he did exactly the same material in the second half as he'd done in the first, just to see how long it would take for the audience to complain.

Nick Hancock and I, along with an act called the Teddy Bear Torturer, did a gig in far-flung Barnstaple in Devon, in a local nightclub – a totally unsuitable venue. Because we were well on time, probably even early, once we crossed the county border into Devon, we decided to stop at every pub en route and have a drink. I think we managed about twelve.

By the time we got to the gig, we were completely rat-arsed. The show was terrible. We were separated from the audience by the dance floor and it felt like a stand-off rather than a stand-up comedy gig. Nick ended up taking off his shoes and throwing them at a couple of hecklers and when it was my turn, I was so pissed I started crying and refused to go on. Some sensible fellow ignored my wimpishness and just pushed me on to the stage, whereupon I probably performed the worst, most unintelligible set of my life to quite a lot of pointing and booing. Happy days.

Sometimes work could be very lonely. I was once sent up to a gig in Tamworth on my own. In those days there was no glamour attached to gigging, no posh hotels or tour manager or driver. I was booked into a pub for the night and when I walked into the bar everyone turned round and stared at me like I was an alien from another planet. The woman behind the bar gave me a key to a very dingy room with just a bed and a bedside table. She said, 'You've got to be back by eleven or we'll lock you out.'

Mmm, what a friendly welcome. I did the gig, which was shit, in a church hall full of people who looked like they'd rather be at a Tory Party knees-up. I got back to the pub at five to eleven, bought seven bottles of Pils, poured them down my neck one by one and slipped into a stupefied sleep. I have never been so depressed in my life.

One of my favourite nights ever was when I was booked to do a gig at the Institute of Contemporary Arts in central London. The place had a slight reputation at the time of being up itself and what happened on the night I worked there seemed to support that.

While I was on stage, a patient I'd known for a long

time, who really wasn't very well at that point, turned up and stood at the back, stark naked, holding only a mobile phone and talking to someone on a far-off planet. What was amazing was that nobody batted an eyelid. I don't know if they assumed he was a moving piece of art or a waiter or what, but they just let him get on with it.

It was pure coincidence that he was there and he didn't really seem to notice it was me on stage. I made a decision not to intervene at that point. I knew I couldn't manage him on my own, knew he wasn't violent, so I just called his ward and they followed it up and had him back by late that night.

I did eventually get round to doing Jongleurs, and it wasn't a happy evening. I was booked to do the whole weekend and on the Friday night found myself in front of a rowdy crowd containing lots of drunks, including a table of dentists on a stag night. And anyone who thinks that dentists are better behaved than those in less elevated jobs had better think again. These guys were completely out of control and I found myself parrying the normal 'Fat slag' and 'Get your tits out' type heckles. And then one of them got on the table, unzipped his trousers and lobbed out his flaccid penis with the words, 'Suck my cock, you fucking bitch!'

Well, I felt this was beyond the call of duty. So at that point, having done my best, I departed the stage and left them to get on with it.

I foolishly expected the club owner to sympathise with me a tiny bit, but instead he looked at his watch and ticked me off because I had come off stage three minutes early. Once again I invited someone to stuff their job . . . yes, you know where it's going, I'm sure. And I've never worked at Jongleurs since.

I spent quite a long time in 1987 sitting in a car on the motorway. At the time, a lot of comics didn't drive and we weren't earning enough to have a driver, so rather than get the train or some hideous coach that made its way round half the country before arriving at the destination, I tended to drive everyone. At least this meant we could all be back home the same night. And most of the time I was working the next day anyway. I must have been absolutely mad, thrashing it up and down the M1 most nights, but at the time it seemed the only way to do it.

One day I had a gig in Nottingham with Bob Mills, Johnny Immaterial and Mandy Knight. You may not have heard of any of these comics, which I find weird, because they are all very funny individuals. I think people assume that the best comics will inevitably make it into the public eye in some way. This is not my experience. There are plenty of brilliant comics who've never surfaced on telly and I'm not sure why. I think it's a combination of luck, identity and being in the right place at the right time. TV execs seem to be looking for a unique characteristic, be it transexualism or grumpiness (although I'm not implying those two go together). And although things are changing, it seems to me that being an Oxford or Cambridge graduate always puts that extra special stamp on your passport into the country of TV.

The Nottingham gig was a problem because my car had broken down and was in the garage. I needed a car fast, so I asked Kristina, my friend with MS. She was happy to lend me her lease car, which had been provided on the basis of her disability. She lived near me and needed it for an early shift in the morning, so I arranged for it to be back by that time. We had a great journey, a good gig and were heading back down the M1 at about one in the morning when we all decided we were hungry and would stop off for an early breakfast at Scratchwood services. Being in an unfamiliar car made the driving slightly more stressful and, as we drove in, I got confused about which car park we should go into and ended up in the lorry park.

This was fine – all I needed to do was turn round and find the right car park – but then I realised a bloody great juggernaut was backing slowly towards us. Two problems: I was unfamiliar with the reverse gear on my friend's car and I couldn't find the horn, which was not in the middle of the steering wheel but at the end of one of those stalks sticking out from the side of the steering wheel. Everyone in the car was shouting and trying to offer advice. The lights were flashing, the windscreen wipers were going and yet nothing seemed to discourage the bloody great machine from edging ever nearer.

Eventually, there was an appalling crunch and it hit us. Thankfully, the driver felt the collision and stopped. However, the damage had been done. The radiator was punctured, the headlights smashed and a bit of concertina-ing had occurred. We got out of the car to talk to the driver and discovered that, in true sitcom style, he was French and didn't speak any English. We did our best to summon our schoolboy and schoolgirl French, to no avail. Details were not exchanged and eventually we gave up and disconsolately headed off, but not before we'd had a bloody massive fry-up to cheer ourselves up. I was forced to phone poor Kristina at 2 a.m. and tell her that I had totalled her car. She was remarkably sanguine about it and I said I would sort out the repairs. Although it wasn't really driveable, we limped home in it and prayed we wouldn't be pulled over by the police for lack of headlights.

Of course, the comedy outcome to this story was that I discovered that I was not actually insured to drive the car and would have to pay for it myself. And a whacking great 600 quid is not an easy sum to lay your hands on if you're a nurse.

One strange side effect of so-called celebrity is the recognition thing and the fact that the press and paparazzi make the excuse that celebrities wanted to be famous so they should put up with what they get. Most people who do the job I do have absolutely no idea that what they are doing will lead to fame or celebrity of any sort, and therefore they are as surprised as anyone when it happens.

My overriding wish had been to be a comic and it had never really occurred to me that it would lead anywhere, but in early 1988, I got a call asking me to come and audition for a show called *Friday Night Live*. This was a sort of comedy and music variety show presented by Ben Elton and there were slots available for new comics. I went to a rehearsal studio in Brixton and did my stuff in the middle of the day, in front of a trio of what appeared to be singularly unimpressed TV people.

However, they decided to book me and when it hit me that I was actually going to be on telly, I wondered how appropriate it would be for me to continue working in a psychiatric emergency clinic. I decided to leave my job, give it six months and if I wasn't able to support myself after that time, I would go back to being a nurse and stop entertaining this silly ambition to make people laugh.

It somehow seemed easier than my other unfulfilled ambitions to be prime minister, become a model, or sail the Atlantic single-handed in a picnic basket.

JO BRAND

The More You Ignore Me

For Alice, the big bad monster wasn't green and hiding under the bed, it sat in the kitchen saying 'bollocks' a lot.

Prone to psychotic episodes, or 'on the road to bonkersville' as Alice's dad would say, Alice's mum Gina isn't easy to live with. Her unpredictable outbursts make life in their little Herefordshire cottage rather eventful.

As 'family' means a mentally ill mother, a hippy father and grandparents who enjoy a drink or five, it's not surprising Alice needs someone to help her through. Thank god she has found someone special . . .

Unfortunately, Alice's special someone is Morrissey of The Smiths, and the closest she's got to him so far is watching him on *Top of the Pops*. But that could all be about to change . . .

Praise for Jo Brand's novels:

'A wonderfully funny and inventive novel' Stephen Fry

'What the hell, pass me one of life's cream cakes – that new book by Jo Brand will do' *Guardian*

'A smart stylist with a confident narrative voice. An accomplished comedy of romantic bad manners' *Observer*

978 0 7553 2232 9

headline
review

JO BRAND

It's Different for Girls

Rachel and Susan do *not* like to be beside the seaside. Hastings is so *uncool*.

Plunging headfirst into the choppy waters of adolescence, they are determined to survive their teens by sticking together. It's a rollercoaster ride of nutty parents, randy language students, stoned hippies, all-night parties on the pier, and an amusement arcade of emotional neediness.

But then Dave, sophisticated art student and unobtainable older boyfriend, enters their lives and everything changes between them. But when the girls find themselves together in London, they discover that their dreams of sex, drugs and rock 'n' roll don't quite match the reality . . .

Praise for Jo Brand's novels:

'A wonderfully funny and inventive novel' Stephen Fry

'A smart stylist with a confident narrative voice. An accomplished comedy of romantic bad manners' *Observer*

'There isn't one dull passage. You could open the book at random, throw a dart and find something droll, well-observed and hard to forget' *Sunday Express*

978 0 7553 2230 5

headline
review

JO BRAND

Sorting Out Billy

Sarah is besotted with Billy, her unpredictable boyfriend. But after another outburst of his bad temper, Sarah's friends Martha and Flower decide that enough is enough. What should they do? Reason with him? Send him to anger management classes? Hire a hit man?

Martha and Flower have issues too. Martha is pregnant by three possible blokes, and hippy Flower's career as a stand-up comic is more sit-down-and-weep after a tongue-lashing by London's finest hecklers.

Can Martha survive single motherhood on a council estate in need of a peace-keeping force? Will Flower find the perfect put-down? And will they sort out Billy before he gets to them first?

Praise for Jo Brand's novels:

'A laugh-a-page tale . . . highly readable and genuinely funny' Alan Davies

'A smart stylist with a confident narrative voice. An accomplished comedy of romantic bad manners' *Observer*

'There isn't one dull passage. You could open the book at random, throw a dart and find something droll, well-observed and hard to forget' *Sunday Express*

978 0 7553 2030 1

headline
review